T0271333

Art of Modern Oriental Management

Applying the Chinese, Japanese and Korean
Management Styles at Work

Art of Modern Oriental Management

Applying the Chinese, Japanese and Korean Management Styles at Work

YU Sing Ong
Southern University College, Malaysia

WS Professional

NEW JERSEY · LONDON · SINGAPORE · BEIJING · SHANGHAI · HONG KONG · TAIPEI · CHENNAI · TOKYO

Published by

WS Professional, an imprint of
World Scientific Publishing Co. Pte. Ltd.
5 Toh Tuck Link, Singapore 596224
USA office: 27 Warren Street, Suite 401-402, Hackensack, NJ 07601
UK office: 57 Shelton Street, Covent Garden, London WC2H 9HE

Library of Congress Cataloging-in-Publication Data
Names: Yu, Sing Ong, author.
Title: Art of modern oriental management : applying the Chinese, Japanese and Korean
    management styles at work / Yu Sing Ong, Southern University College, Malaysia.
Description: New Jersey : World Scientific, [2017] |
    Includes bibliographical references and index.
Identifiers: LCCN 2017006624| ISBN 9789813220317 (hardcover) |
    ISBN 9789813220324 (softcover)
Subjects: LCSH: Management--Asia.
Classification: LCC HD70.A7 Y83 2017 | DDC 658.00951--dc23
LC record available at https://lccn.loc.gov/2017006624

British Library Cataloguing-in-Publication Data
A catalogue record for this book is available from the British Library.

First published 2017
Reprinted in India: 2017

Desk Editor: Jiang Yulin

Typeset by Stallion Press
Email: enquiries@stallionpress.com

Printed in Singapore

To my lovely wife,
Jesslyn,
and my two loving daughters,
Yvonne and Michelle

Contents

Preface

This book aims to present an overview of Chinese, Japanese and Korean modern management styles. It discusses various case studies in China, Japan and Korea and attempts to give some insights of the decision-making processes of the CEOs of these companies. The cultures of these countries are influenced by Confucianism, Daoism and Buddhism. As such, there are some basic similarities in their management styles. The ancient military strategist, Sun Tzu, had taught many strategies and concepts which are being adapted to modern-day management. The internationalisation of Chinese, Japanese and Korean companies have blurred the lines of distinction between Western and Eastern management styles. The need for Western managers to adapt to Asian way of doing business, and likewise for Asian companies to understand Western business practices, means that managers have to bridge the gaps and adopt the best management practices containing both Western and Eastern elements.

Asian management is not as unique or different from Western management styles as most other authors portray. The various cases discussed in this book show that the various Asian honchos have blended both Western and Oriental styles in their management strategies. Many of them have received their education from Western universities. Asian managers are increasingly taking a more pragmatic approach in their management style, not by choice but by necessity, as they seek to manoeuvre through a constantly changing business environment. They will maintain, adapt and adopt whatever aspects of Western and Eastern management styles that proved advantageous to them.

Much of Chinese management's approach in Sun Tzu's *Art of War* is of conceptual in nature. It does not provide a step-by-step analysis of the processes to follow nor does it provide a framework to guide the novice manager. The author tries to complement the broad based theories of Sun Tzu and other Eastern concepts with certain Western management frameworks and analytical tools. By providing a multifaceted approach to understanding modern Oriental management, the author stresses the complexities of the business environment in China, Japan and Korea. This book offers valuable insights of the management styles of Oriental managers by providing a critical perspective of their thought processes in simple but highly relevant illustrations of models and frameworks.

Business people, academicians and students will get a deeper understanding of Oriental management practices from reading this book through the discussions of various case studies. The author suggests that Western theories of management are applicable to Eastern cultural context with some adaptations to the local environment. Through the use of explanatory Western models, the author has developed rigorous decision-making rules for Eastern ideologies. Asian CEOs are becoming more flexible and quick to adjust their management styles to remain competitive in the globalised economies. With this book, business leaders and managers are able to apply the best of Chinese, Japanese and Korean management practices to their daily work.

The eight sections of this book cover:

1) Influences of Philosophy and Religion
2) Cultural Sensitivities

3) Chinese Management Styles
4) Sun Tzu Art of War of Modern Management
5) Japanese Management Styles
6) Korean Management Styles
7) Comparison of Management Styles
8) West Learning from East

Acknowledgements

I would like to thank Professor Wong Yoon Wah for his encouragement and support to me in writing this book. He has been a great motivator and mentor to me. I would also like to extend my appreciation to Dr Thock Kiah Wah who has provided me with an exciting insight into his unique Oriental management style. I also wish to express my deepest thanks to Professor Phua Kok Khoo, Chua Hong Koon and their team at World Scientific Publishing for their guidance in launching this book.

About the Author

Associate Professor Sing Ong Yu has over 29 years of senior management experience in banking, research, consulting and education. He started his career in Wall Street, New York, in the 1980s. Following his return to Singapore, he was instrumental in establishing and managing the Investment Management unit of a pension fund. He was also the Research Director of a major local bank and the Regional Vice President of Investment Banking of an international bank.

As an entrepreneur, Associate Professor Yu had established three companies in consultancy, project management and education. He had provided advisory services to over 500 private and public companies in Singapore, Philippines, Thailand, Malaysia, Vietnam and Indonesia.

His desire to share his knowledge and experiences led him to join the education industry in 2004. He had managed three universities in Vietnam and Malaysia and an education institution in Singapore. Associate Professor Yu graduated with a Doctorate in Business and a Doctorate in Arts Management. He is also a Certified Financial Planner in Malaysia.

Associate Professor Yu is also the author of *Dao of Managing Higher Education in Asia*, a publication by World Scientific Publishing, Singapore.

Section 1

Influences of Philosophy and Religion

Confucianism

onfucius (551 B.C.–479 B.C.) had a great influence on Chinese culture. He advocated the concept of *ren* ("humanity", "humanness", "goodness" or "benevolence"). Confucius also viewed individuals as a social being whose identity derives from his interaction with the broader human community. He preached personal virtues, social order and respect for elders. *Ren* encompasses qualities such as self-discipline, humility, loyalty, courage and trustworthiness.

Mencius (Meng Ke or Meng Zi), born in 372 B.C. carried on Confucius' philosophy. He introduced the concept of democracy by emphasising that subjects are more important the rulers. He also advocated that one's character needed to be moulded by education. On leadership, Mencius emphasised that a wise leader is one who portrays benevolence and righteousness.

Mencius said:

> "If a king shares the worries and concerns of his subjects and makes policies that enable them to live and work in peace and contentment, there is no force in existence that can stop him uniting the world." (Xu & Zhang, 2007)

Mencius believed that individuals are good by nature and that it is society's bad influence that causes bad moral characters. This assertion put Mencius in greater agreement with Daoism than with Confucianism. While this may seem paradoxical, Confucius himself did not provide any theory on human nature and/or elaborate why a person should be moral.

Confucianism focuses on the manner human beings ought to behave in society according to ethical or moral ways. It does not offer any explanations on the relationships between human beings and Nature. By overly emphasising on human ideals or standards, it can be argued that Confucianism has placed too much emphasis on worldly goals.

Daoists realise that human beings are only a miniscule part of the larger process of Nature. Human nature in its original pristine form can only be understood to be "so of itself" (*ziran* or naturalness). When human nature is aligned with Nature, order and harmony are the results.

In Daoism, self-cultivation is an important element in the search for meaning of human nature. Through self-cultivation, a Daoist seeks to return to a state of existence which is in harmony with Nature. Selfishness and ill intentions often result in disharmonies and unintended consequences which are against the natural rhythms of Nature.

From this perspective, the author postulates that Daoism had influenced Mencius' views on human nature. Mencius believed that human nature is good as it is one's innate tendencies to be benevolent, self-righteous, and proprietous. "Evil", on the other hand, is not inborn but something artificial from outside. Mencius asserted that serious efforts need to be made to return to one's original nature. This return to one's original nature is synonymous to the concept of self-cultivation in Daoism.

Confucianism focuses on moral character and ethics which encompass Five Constants or *wu chang* (五常). They are:

1. *Ren* (仁), humaneness, benevolence;
2. *Yi* (义), righteousness, justice;

3. *Li* (礼), proper rite;
4. *Zhi* (智), knowledge, wisdom;
5. *Xin* (信), integrity.

Describing *ren*, Confucius advised "not to do to others as you would not wish done to yourself". He believed that man is kind and good by nature and should not seek wealth and status at the expense of humanity. A Confucian manager is expected to display goodness towards others and manage with kindness.

Yi, an ethical orientation of Confucianism, refers to the moral dispositions to do good. Individuals should have the ability to recognise what is right and good. Certain actions have to be taken for the sole reason they are right regardless of the outcomes. In this respect, managers are expected to uphold the highest standards of moral conduct.

The Confucian concept of *li* refers to rituals or appropriate behaviours and roles. *Li* promotes ideals such as filial piety, faith and loyalty. Illustrating the broader application of *li*, Confucius included broad topics such as learning, titles and governance. *Li* regulates human interactions and etiquettes and lays the basis for the principles of social order.

Mencius added the concept of *Zhi* to Confucianism. *Zhi* refers to moral wisdom and knowing right from wrong. According to Mencius, "evil" could originate from lack of knowledge of external circumstances. *Zhi* is part of the growing maturation of an individual as wisdom comes with age.

Xin refers to keeping one's words and being faithful. Faithfulness is an indispensable virtue for a person. A man without faith could not be entrusted to carry out important tasks. Trust is an utmost important virtue of a leader as honest and faithful leaders are needed to maintain a harmonious organisation.

Face-saving is an important Chinese business concept which could be traced back to Confucius. *Lian* (face) reflects one's standing in public. Criticism from another party to cause one to lose face may jeopardise the business relationships between the parties.

Confucius believed that education should be provided to all without any discrimination. According to him, education can make a difference to a person's character. One of the most important contributions of Confucius is that he advocated that all humans are equal and of one class.

Confucius said:

"When you see a worthy person, endeavor to emulate him. When you see an unworthy person, then examine your inner self."

Confucius advocated the five relationships model to determine ruler–subject, father–son, husband–wife, elder brother–younger brother and friend–friend relationships (Figure 1). Because of the hierarchical nature, titles are important. Chinese (including Japanese and Koreans) address each other by the appropriate titles: "Mr Wong", "President Lee" or "General Ng".

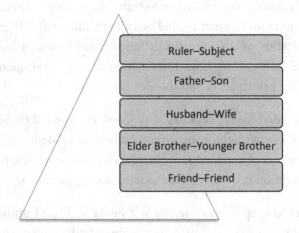

Figure 1: Confucianism on Relationships

Chapter

2

Confucian Influences
on Modern Management

Much of Confucius' ideology could be applicable in modern-day management practices.

Confucius said:

1) *"Success depends upon previous preparation, and without such preparation there is sure to be failure."*

   Businesses have to be sufficiently prepared to face the challenges in the global environment. Managers have to constantly conduct scenario planning exercises to ensure that they are adequately prepared for any downturns.

2) *"If you think in terms of a year, plant a seed; if in terms of 10 years, plant trees; if in terms of 100 years, teach the people."*

   Confucius highlighted the importance of formulating strategies to develop competitive advantage in the business. This strategic plan is to be put into action through proper planning and organisation.

3) *"Better a diamond with a flaw than a pebble without."*

    Managers should value righteousness and ethical principles above profits. Their business behaviours should be governed by high moral and ethical principles.

4) *"Let the ruler be a ruler, the subject a subject, a father a father, and a son a son."*

    The concept of absolute loyalty towards one's organisation is becoming increasingly unpopular. As employees become more educated and exposed to Western management styles, their demands for greater recognition of their work performances increase. Increased competition for talents means that the mobility rate of employees also increases. The expectation that employees work tirelessly for the good of the organisation and the nation as stated in the *Analects of Confucius* seems unrealistic in modern times as employees are now inclined towards work-life balance.

Mencius' contribution to modern-day management is in the area of *participative management* and *employee autonomy*. He stressed that leaders should also learn from their subordinates.

Mencius said:

"Today there are many states, all equal in size and virtue, none being able to dominate the others. This is simply because the rulers are given to employing those they can teach rather than those from whom they can learn."

Mencius also taught the need for good interpersonal relationship between superior and subordinate. Managers have to earn the support and respect of their subordinates if they wish to achieve greater goals.

Mencius quoted:

"You can never gain the Empire without the heartfelt admiration of the people in it."

Mencius' teaching could be illustrated in the diagram below. He saw a good leader as possessing three main qualities: benevolence, servant-leadership, and humanism (Figure 2).

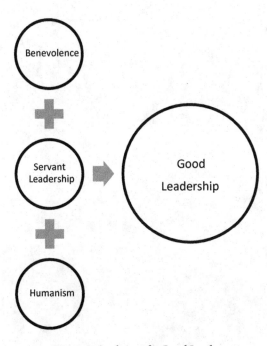

Figure 2: Qualities of a Good Leader

3

Daoism

Daoism was founded by Lao Zi (original name Li Er), a contemporary of Confucius. Lao Zi wrote the *Dao De Jing*, the famous Chinese philosophical text which consists of 5,000 words and 81 chapters. The concept of *Dao* and *De* are ambiguous as Lao Zi employed paradoxical languages to present his teachings. As such, *Dao De Jing* is open to a variety of interpretations. *Dao* and *De* have been translated as *way* and *virtue*. A number of themes in *Dao De Jing* are applicable to modern-day management. These include: the need to avoid conflict, the need to maintain balance and harmony, and the need to pursue inner-self cultivation.

In Daoism, balance or harmony is inherent in nature. Through multiple transformations by and within nature, things come to life. The transformation process is believed to be natural with no external forces involved. This concept has important implications in modern Chinese management as it signifies that the business environment is constantly changing and that companies need to adapt to these changes. As the environment changes, new business opportunities are also being created.

Dao De Jing is more than just a philosophical text. It is applicable to politics, cosmology, aesthetics and ethics. Lao Zi believed that it is best to let nature take its course without human intervention. This is evident in the opening phrase of the first chapter of *Dao De Jing*:

> *"The truth that may be told is not the everlasting truth. The name given to a thing is not the everlasting Name."*

Lao Zi advocated that *not doing* or *non-action* was the best way to avoid active intervention. This core principle has significant influences on Chinese management style such as motivating employees, and not controlling them.

> *"The sage puts himself last and becomes the first,*
> *Neglects himself, and is preserved*
> *Is it not because he is unselfish that he fulfils himself?"*

> *Dao De Jing*

Chapter 4

Modern Daoism's Application in Business

In the modern world, Daoism is a global religious tradition characterised by cultural, ethnic and international diversity. Daoist followers value *wuzhi* (non-knowing), and at the same time, seek to resolve *huo* (perplexity). The *Dao* (Way) is formless, nameless, mysterious, and unknowable. While unknowable, the *Dao* may be experienced and pervades the world and being. This perplexity leads one to commit to search for deeper understanding.

Daoism is often regarded as both philosophy and religion. The philosophical aspect of Daoism is related to *Dao De Jing* (Scripture of the Dao and Inner Power) and *Zhuangzi* (Book of Master Zhuang). The practice of *wu wei* (non-action) reflects self-transformation that is inherent within things, as all natural processes are perceived to be linked to harmony and balance. This concept of *wu wei* has often been criticised as being overly simplistic and impractical in modern-day management theory. Transformation occurs naturally with no external force involved. Transformation also means that things are never absolute and constantly changing. Another principle of Daoism is reversion which implies that the opposite things can occur.

In Daoism, the two polar energies of Ying and Yang represent the principle of natural and complementary forces. They are opposite forces that fit together seamlessly and work together in harmony. Ying and Yang are not static as the balance ebbs and flows between them. This is implied in the curvature line where they meet. The concept of Ying and Yang is also applicable to business (Figure 3).

Figure 3: Daoism for Business

The influence of Daoism is prevalent in contemporary Chinese businesses (Tian, 2008; Xing and Sims, 2011). The perplexed situation of mingling philosophies and religions contributes much to the development of China's management theory today (Wang *et al.*, 2012). The principle of transformation means that alternatives and other opportunities are available and that things are never absolute (Cheung and Chan, 2005).

The principle of reversion advocates a reverse action and using a soft approach such as "give in order to take, and follow in order to lead" (Cheung and Chan, 2008).

"When one is about to take an inspiration, he is sure to make a (previous) expiration; when he is going to weaken another, he will first strengthen him; when he is going to overthrow another, he will first have raised him up; when he is going to despoil another, he will first have made gifts to him: this is called 'Hiding the light (of his procedure)'.

The soft overcomes the hard; and the weak the strong.

Fishes should not be taken from the deep; instruments for the profit of a state should not be shown to the people."

Dao De Jing

Loyalty is not important in Daoism as it advocates following the *Way* rather than following instructions of a company's boss. This is unlike Confucianism which places great importance on loyalty, order and respect. In Daoism, living in simplicity and in tune with nature is more important. To Daoist adherents, the best form of governance is the one that governs the least. In modern management context, this relates to empowerment and delegation of duties and responsibilities to subordinates. The humanistic approach of Daoism opens up new perspectives in leadership studies and could provide complementary answers to Western models which are often empirically based, but do not provide explanations of relational processes.

Lao Zi said:

"If people are difficult to govern, it is because those in authority are too fond of action."

Modern Chinese management style is a synthesis of Confucianism, Daoism, Buddhism and Occidental philosophies. This is a result of advancements in technologies and globalisation of Asian economies as business people and academicians become more exposed to other cultures and adopt those management practices that offer the best results and solutions to them.

Chapter

5

Buddhism

Buddhism originated from India and shares many of the Hindu concepts of *karma* and *samsara*. The founder was a young prince from Nepal named Siddhartha Gautama. He left a life of luxury to experience human sufferings. After attaining enlightenment, he was known as Buddha and spread his religious teachings of Buddhism.

According to Hinduism, *karma* governs the universe and the beings within it. Some beings are being elevated to the upper planetary systems while others are being lowered into the lower planetary systems. The sum total of one's good and bad deeds will determine how one will be rewarded or punished in the next life. The belief of *samara* or reincarnation means that there is a never ending cycle of birth, death and rebirth.

Buddhism spread into China during the Han dynasty. The popular branch of Buddhism in China is Mahayana. The Buddha that is generally worshipped is Amitabha and the Buddha which is about to arrive is Maitreya or Mi-Le Buddha. The popular Bodhisattva is Avalokiteshvara or Guanyin, also known as the Goddess of Mercy. Buddhism in China became popular under the Chan school which emphasized meditation. Chan Buddhism later spread to Japan where it is known as Zen Buddhism.

Today, Buddhism also plays a large role in shaping the business practices of many Asian managers. An aphorism from Buddha states:

"You can only lose what you cling to."

Buddha reminded that change is everywhere and nothing is permanent. Managers should embrace change and detach from the dogmas of old management styles.

Buddhism has its practical application in today's business world (Figure 4). Its focuses on communal harmony, ethics, teamwork, learning and development, and employers' duties are important in shaping modern management practices in the Orient.

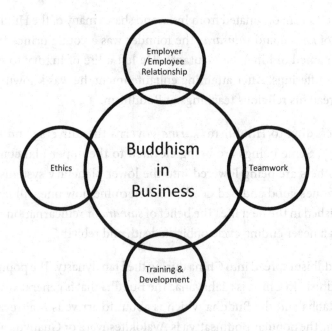

Figure 4: Buddhism in Business

Buddhism also advocates constant learning and development. The development of others is equally important as the development of self.

Buddha said:

"Believe nothing merely because you have been told it. Do not believe what your teacher tells you merely out of respect for the teacher. But whatever, after due examination and analysis, you find to be kind, conducive to the good, the benefit, the welfare of all beings — that doctrine believe and cling to, and take it as your guide."

Buddha in his advice to Sigalaka Sutta enumerates five ways an employer should treat his employees:

1) Assigning work according to their strengths — The work assigned should be according to their mental and physical strengths. Bosses should not take advantage of their employees.
2) Giving them food and wages — Pay them accordingly to their efforts.
3) Tending them in sickness — Grant them medical leave when they are unwell.
4) Sharing with them unusual delicacies — Reward them with bonuses or other material means.
5) Granting leave at suitable times — Grant them time off for their personal matters.

Teamwork is an important concept in Buddhism. Personal sacrifice for the benefit of the team helps the organisation to pull through in times of crisis. Buddha said:

"Whoever offers sacrifice, or whoever gets others to do so — all these are following a course of merit benefiting many others."

Case of Robert Kuok

One of the most successful Hong Kong tycoon, Robert Kuok, had mentioned that the biggest influence on his life was his devoutly Buddhist mother. She had taught him to uphold high moral standards in the process of making money and to avoid businesses that bring harm to society. Humility was also one of his greatest secret for success. He has also tried to pass on these set of values to the younger generation.

Today, the Kuok Group of companies includes the unlisted Kerry Group, Shangri La Asia and Wilmar International, which is the largest processor of palm oil in the world.

The secret of Robert Kuok's success could be found in some of his own words and the words of his business partners and competitors.

Robert Kuok once said:

"I adapt like a chameleon to the particular society where I am operating at the moment."

Robert Riley of Mandarin Oriental Hotel Group, a Shangri La competitor, said:

"He's a local everywhere he goes."

John Farrell of Coca Cola, a business partner, said:

"His whole life has been built around building networks with overseas Chinese and in China. Kerry's ability to do things fast is incredible."

As mentioned earlier, one of Robert Kuok's secrets to success was humility. He claimed that he preferred people with an inner humility than one who portrayed that he knew a lot. Someone with humility is ready to acknowledge his weaknesses but at the same time willing to manage them. This is the key to his political astuteness.

Lao Tzu said:

"Knowing others is wisdom, knowing yourself is Enlightenment."

While the Kuok Group of companies has significant lesser investments in Western countries as compared to China, Robert Kuok's ability of getting things done fast is an envy of other business leaders, both Eastern and Western. He has been described by Forbes as one of the shrewdest businessmen in the world.

Robert Kuok has successfully managed to integrate the qualities of Eastern and Western management styles together. Western management styles are more action oriented while Eastern management styles advocate more contemplation than fast action.

Balancing clarity with ambiguity requires a high degree of mental discipline which Robert Kuok seems to possess. Too much inquiry and deliberation result in taking too much time to make decisions. Conversely, spending too little time on inquiry and deliberation may result in the wrong decision being made (Figure 5).

Figure 5: Clarity and Ambiguity

Case of Wahaha Beverage

Wahaha is the largest beverage company in China with 70 production bases and 30,000 employees. The company was founded by Zong Qinghou in 1987. Chairman Zong's management style is leading with authority yet displaying benevolence. He believes that Chinese companies need strong leaders who are open-minded and tolerant to employees. Employees should be given a second chance to learn from their mistakes.

In 1999, the company established a stock option scheme to reward employees who have worked for more than one year. Employees are also given subsidies to purchase affordable houses in Hangzhou. The school fees of children of employees are also paid by the company. Chairman Zong believes that these are some ways to motivate employees to work for the company. Most employees work for the company till retirement. The company strongly emphasises on its motto "love your small family, develop our big family, and serve the country".

While Chairman Zong is ranked as one of China's richest men, he is, nevertheless, a frugal person. In an interview with BBC News in 2011, Chairman Zong claimed that he lived on USD20 a day. He said:

"My only exercise is doing market research...."

The statement reflects Chairman Zong's seriousness in his work as he seeks to balance depth and breadth in understanding the market. Too much breadth results in too little analysis done on a particular issue. Conversely, making too much in-depth analysis of a particular problem results in one ignoring alternative solutions (Figure 6).

Chairman Zong makes all the decisions. The 18 functional heads have very little decision-making capabilities. He sees himself as a paternal figure, regarding his employees as his children.

As in many entrepreneur-owned business, control of the company lies in the hands of family members. His wife and daughter help run some important divisions of the group business. Chairman Zong believes that hard work is the only way to get someone out of poverty and does not advocate simply giving money away. He once said in an interview:

"Donation is not charity. A true philanthropist should be able to help people in need by continuously creating social wealth."

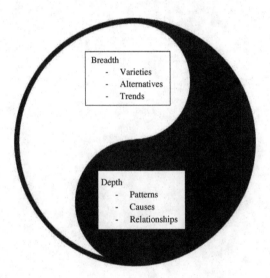

Figure 6: Balancing Depth and Breadth

Chapter

6

Contribution of Confucianism, Daoism and Buddhism to Modern Oriental Management

Figure 7 shows the contribution of Confucianism, Daoism and Buddhism to modern Oriental management. Managers may adopt a combination of various philosophies in their management styles. For example, they may value the corporate hierarchy, yet they may empower their subordinates and advocate change management. Today's modern Oriental management is a fusion of Oriental philosophies and Western theories.

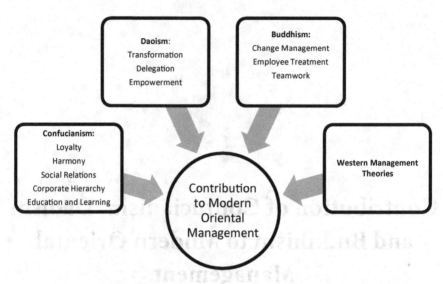

Figure 7: Contribution to Modern Oriental Management

Case of Jack Ma of Alibaba Group

The Chairman of the Alibaba Group, Jack Ma, is one renowned businessman who has incorporated elements of Confucianism, Daoism, Buddhism and Western management theories into his management style. At Alibaba, the culture of accommodation and transformation, learning and development, teamwork, respect for hierarchy, motivating talents and performance management are all weaved together to form a unique corporate culture.

Jack Ma advocates using Chinese culture as a foundation while adapting Western principles. He believes in providing overall guidance while letting his ground-level managers decide how they would like to run the company. By empowering the managers, they become more motivated and able to make their own decisions rather than relying on him for direction. Increased levels of satisfaction lead to higher employees' loyalty (Wagner & Harter, 2006).

It is essential for Jack Ma to balance long-term *goal orientation* with *engagement*. Focusing too much on goals will result in shutting out others' opinion, leading to a myopic self-centred view of the organisation. Conversely, too much engagement will result in too many opinions, leading to delays in making decisions (Figure 8).

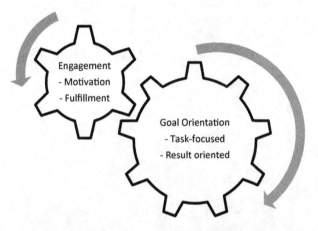

Figure 8: Balancing Long-Term Goals and Engagement

Section 2

Cultural Sensitivities

Chapter

7

Cultural Dimensions

Managers need to develop the awareness of other cultures. This usually involves internal changes of attitudes and values. For international managers to be successful in another culture, they have to understand how culture affects work and organisational processes (Johnson, 1998; Francesco & Gold, 2005; Khatri, 2009).

Hofstede (1983a) conducted cultural studies on IBM's operations in 70 countries and mapped key cultural characteristics according to four value dimensions (Figure 9):

(1) *Power distance* relates to the acceptance that power is distributed unequally. High power distance means that the organisation is highly autocratic and that employees have very little decision-making opportunities.
(2) *Uncertainty avoidance* refers to the degree in which members of a society feel uncomfortable with risk and uncertainty.
(3) *Individualism versus Collectivism* is the degree to which people feel that they are independent from others.

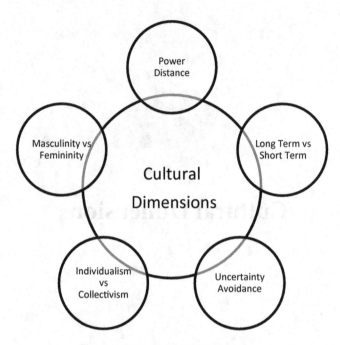

Figure 9: Hofstede Cultural Dimensions

(4) *Masculinity versus Femininity* is attributed to dominant values of society such as assertiveness, acquisition of wealth, and quality of life in the case of the former. Conversely, *femininity* refers to the softer values such as relationships, caring and quality of life.

(5) *Long term versus short term* relates to fostering of virtues oriented towards future rewards, perseverance and thrift (Hofstede & Bond, 1980).

Chinta and Capar (2007) noted that managers in the United States demonstrated more individualism than Chinese managers. They were also low on power distance and uncertainty avoidance as compared to their Chinese counterparts. They felt that they were in control of situations and could bring about changes in their organisations.

Managers should not allow cultural differences to form the basis for criticism and biasness. It is how they deal with these differences that make a difference. While Oriental cultures of China, Japan and Korea have been

Westernised, they still contain strong values of humility and modesty. Part of the reason for this Westernisation of Occidental cultures is the large foreign direct investments pouring into China, Japan and Korea over the years.

According to the World Investment Report 2015, China was the world's largest Foreign Direct Investments recipient, surpassing the United States. This huge increase inward flow FDI was due to the opening up of China to the outside world. A total of USD135 billion flowed into China in 2015. In the same year, China's outbound FDI reached almost USD127 billion.

8

Understanding Oriental Business Culture

A n understanding of cross-cultural management issues is essential for a foreign company to penetrate the host country market. This understanding is even more important if the foreign firm chooses to establish an operation in the host country as it may require different organisational structures and human resource management policies. Managers need to be acquainted with specific cultural issues so that they can make better decisions and avoid unnecessary conflicts and losses.

Businesses in China, Korea and Japan emphasize more on building relations or *guanxi* as the formula for a long lasting relationship. The foreign firm needs to have an understanding of issues relating to language, behaviour, rituals, labour relations, workforce attitudes, and consumer preferences. If managed properly, a multicultural work environment can promote workplace learning as it facilitates exchange of new ideas between colleagues from different backgrounds.

Case of Starbucks

One foreign company that understands Chinese business culture is Starbucks. The company has 2,100 stores across 100 cities. In Shanghai alone, there are 300 stores. It has a Chinese CEO, Belinda Wong, for its China's operations. Starbucks China also pays special attention in its employees. It has announced that it would subsidise housing accommodations for an estimated 7,000 employees. In 2014, the company introduced the China Youth Development Program aimed at training college students to be future leaders. Starbucks CEO, Howard Schultz, mentioned that he would not be surprised if one day Starbucks has more stores in China than in the United States.

While the company faces competition from new generations of tea houses and other coffee-houses with a laid-back environment much like Starbucks, its success in China can be attributed to a number of factors. These include:

(1) Having the right partners in different regions of the market. The company partners with Beijing's Mei Da company for the Northern region, Taiwan's Uni-President Group in the Eastern region, and Hong Kong's Maxim's Group in the Southern region.

(2) Brand integrity as Starbucks ensures that the quality of its products and services is maintained. Starbucks has sent some of its best baristas to train new employees to ensure that each store meets global standards.

(3) Capitalising on local tea-drinking culture by introducing local ingredients such as green tea frappuccino, red bean muffins, and mooncakes on its menu.

(4) At the same time, Starbucks provides a stage of social status for its customers. Its customers feel that they are hip and sophisticated and able to afford to pay USD5 for a cup of coffee.

(5) Starbucks has leveraged on social media effectively. The company has set up a Weibo account where its customers are able to post images

of themselves with friends. In addition, it has also launched a WeChat campaign where customers can have access to exclusive content with coupons and other promotions.

(6) Starbucks takes an interest in every employee well-being. It encourages learning of employees which in turn motivates them to work harder for the company. The Corporate Headquarters is called Starbucks Support Centre which reflects its role of providing support rather than functioning as an autocratic decision-making body (Gulati *et al.*, 2008). Through decentralisation of its global businesses, Starbucks is able to adapt to local social-cultural factors.

The company seems to have discovered the right formula for the Chinese market while others such as Facebook, Google, Yahoo, Adobe, Apple and Microsoft have either closed their China's operations fully or partially.

Case of Adidas

Adidas plans to open 3,000 stores in China by 2020, expanding its existing 9,000 outlets to 12,000 stores. The company is cautiously optimistic about China's sportswear market which grew by 11% in 2015 to RMB165 billion. Sales in China for Adidas grew 38% to USD2.79 billion and accounted for 15% of its global revenue.

Over 50% of Adidas' products are manufactured in China. In China, its market share of sportswear is 13.8% compared to Nike 14.3%, according to Euromonitor. The company has adopted various strategies to target different segments of the China market. These include:

(1) Multi-brand strategy whereby Adidas introduced sub-brands to cater to customers with different income levels. The "NEO" line is

targeted at teenagers and priced about half the "Originals" line, and helps build brand awareness in lower tier cities.

(2) Internet strategy whereby it worked closely with Tmall.com online store to tap into China's growing e-commerce market. At the same time, the company is also developing its own online store to complement the distribution channel of its Tmall store.

(3) Sponsorship strategy whereby it sponsored major sports events and activities such as the Beijing Marathon.

In June 2016, sports giant Adidas AG signed an agreement with Dalian Wanda Group to promote soccer and basketball in China. The latter had signed a partnership agreement with soccer's governing body FIFA in 2016. Dalian Wanda also invested in a 20% stake in Spanish club Atletico Madrid. Adidas has announced that it plans to add another 3,000 stores to its existing 9,000 stores in China. The company hopes to ride on the government's mandate to make soccer compulsory in schools.

Besides Wanda, four other Chinese companies have acquired stakes in European soccer clubs. Appliance retailer, Suning Commerce Group, paid USD306 million for a stake in Italian club Inter Milan. Recon Group acquired English club Aston Villla for USD95.5 million recently. Rastar Group which manufactures model cars invested between USD15 million to USD19 million in Spanish club Espanyol while United Vansen International Sports took a small USD9 million stake in Dutch club ADO Den Haag.

Local Chinese sportswear companies are also collaborating with international brands to strengthen their home base position. For example, Anta Sports Products with over 9,000 retail outlets in China, Hong Kong and Macau, had formed a joint venture with Japanese skiing brand Descente and Itochu, another sportswear manufacturer. The company has been marketing Fila brand in China since 2009.

The process of building long-term relationships in China requires patience and mutual benefits for both the foreign companies and local partners. In addition, foreign companies have to be seen to develop the Chinese workforce, both at the senior and junior levels (Figure 10).

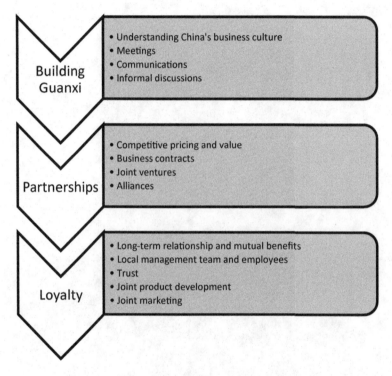

Figure 10: Process of Building Long-Term Relationships

Chapter

9

Failure of Foreign Companies in China

China is the second largest economy in the world and many companies just cannot afford to ignore the vast opportunities that it has to offer. However, many foreign companies make mistakes entering China without fully understanding the market.

Chinese businesses, together with their Japanese and Korean counterparts, view achieving long-term goals as more important than meeting short-term objectives. They prefer harmony and build on accumulated wisdom and intuition rather than reasoning and objectivity (Scarborough, 1988). However, in today's business environment, competitive bidding is gaining popularity. Foreign managers have to be aware that there is no single formula to ensure long-term relationship. They will have to adopt multifaceted approach in their business dealings with clients. While adapting to some of the traditions that are crucial to business successes in the Orient, they also have to offer competitive pricing and distinctive value of their products or services to cement their relationships with the local parties.

It is, therefore, worthwhile for foreign companies to pay special attention to these few issues listed below:

(1) Researching and understanding the markets;
(2) Searching for the right partner;
(3) Obtaining support from the local authorities.

Researching and Understanding the Market

Case of eBay

It is essential for foreign firms to have an understanding of its potential partners and existing competitors. eBay from the United States suffered badly as it did not understand the Chinese online shoppers. Its main competitor was Taobao, a member of the Alibaba group. Taobao had a chat line which enabled buyers to talk to sellers and this helped assuage their concerns. In addition, it offered an Escrow payment feature known as Alipay. Ebay shut down its China site in 2006 after three years of acquiring its China entity, Eachnet.

To further boost its market share, Taobao had launched a new data sharing service which enables small businesses to have access to its huge database of consumer transactions. These small businesses can access industry macro-data to have better understanding of consumer behavioural trend. Such services strengthen Taobao's partnerships with its clients. At the same time, small businesses are increasingly reliant on Taobao for accessing market data information. Figure 11 illustrates the strategies which Taobao had taken against eBay.

Jack Ma said:

"eBay may be a shark in the ocean, but I am a crocodile in the Yangtze River. If we fight in the ocean, we lose — but if we fight in the river, we win."

With an estimated USD15 billion in cash and short-term investments after its IPO, the crocodile is now ready to fight the shark outside the river.

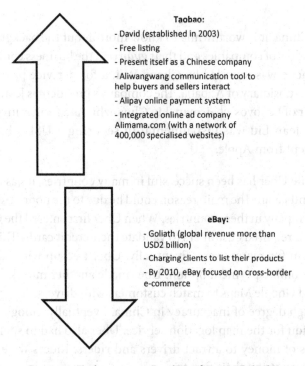

Taobao:
- David (established in 2003)
- Free listing
- Present itself as a Chinese company
- Aliwangwang communication tool to help buyers and sellers interact
- Alipay online payment system
- Integrated online ad company Alimama.com (with a network of 400,000 specialised websites)

eBay:
- Goliath (global revenue more than USD2 billion)
- Charging clients to list their products
- By 2010, eBay focused on cross-border e-commerce

Figure 11: Taobao versus eBay (David versus Goliath)

Choosing the Right Partner

Case of Uber

In August 2016, Uber announced that it is selling its China's operations to rival Didi Chuxing in a landmark deal that sees the company owning 18 percent of Didi. The relationship is complicated as Didi Chuxing had invested USD100 million in Lyft, Uber's largest competitor. Didi–Lyft partnership was expanded to include Grab Taxi in South East Asia and Ola in India, in an effort to stem Uber's regional expansion. Didi Chuxing was formed in 2015 following the merger between Didi Dache and Kuaidi Dache, to compete with Uber. The firm raised USD7 billion in its public listing and counts Apple, Alibaba and Tencent as its shareholders.

In China, it is worthwhile to know more about the background of the founders of companies and their *guanxi* in the business community. Didi Dache was founded by Cheng Wei, a former vice president of Alipay, a subsidiary of Alibaba. The company's president is Jean Liu, the daughter of Lenovos' chairman, Liu Chuanzhi. As a former investment banker, Jean Liu was instrumental in securing a USD1 billion of investment from Apple.

While Uber has been successful in many countries, it has failed in China and Japan. The main reason could be due to the poor positioning of the company in these countries. When Uber first entered the Chinese market, it required customers to validate their credit cards. This posed a problem for many users. Eventually, Uber tied up with Alipay to offer the online payment option. Uber made another mistake when it first used Google Maps to match customers with drivers. Google Maps had a high degree of inaccuracy in China. Eventually, Google tied up with Baidu for the map location service. Uber also had to spend large amounts of money to attract drivers and riders. Riders were offered large discounts on their first trip.

Uber's demise in China was triggered when the Chinese government introduced a national regulation on ride-hailing services. Uber faced regulations from local governments on the issuance of ride-hailing services drivers' licenses and the types of cars that can be driven.

Uber needs to learn that China is a very different market where the company needs a local partner who is familiar with the ride-sharing market in China. The company needs to pay particular attention to the various dimensions of internationalisation if it wishes to continue operating in China (Figure 12).

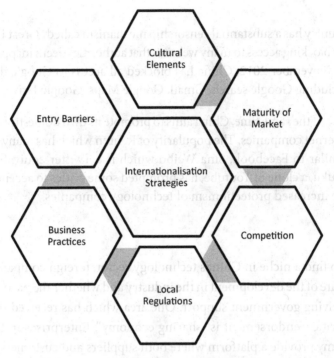

Figure 12: Dimensions of Internationalisation

Building Relationship with the Authorities

Case of Google

The building of good relationship with the Chinese authorities will determine the success or failure of the foreign companies in China. Google's refusal to abide by the regulatory guidelines has caused its services to be blocked in China. The company shut its Chinese search engine in 2010, giving up the huge Chinese market. While Google is experiencing a market share decline, its Chinese competitor, Baidu, has seen a steady increase in its share of the search engine market. Similar fates have fallen on other foreign online sites such as Foursquare and Twitter.

Foreign companies have to abide by Chinese laws which include restrictions on free speech if they wish to do business in China. The country has a substantial censorship mechanism called "Great Firewall" for blocking access to many websites that authorities deem inappropriate. By November 2012, China has blocked all access to Google domains, including Google search, Gmail, Google Maps, Google Drive, etc.

At the same time, China aims to promote its own domestic brands of internet companies. The popularity of Renren which has many features similar to Facebook, Sina Weibo which is a Twitter equivalent, and Youku, a clone of Youtube, has prompted some critics to accentuate on the increased protectionism of technology companies.

To find a niche in China's technology sector, foreign companies need to be aware of the development in the industry and whether the particular sector is receiving government support. One area which has received the Chinese authorities' endorsement is "sharing economy". Enterprises in the sharing economy provide a platform where both suppliers and customers are able to transact deals online. Large companies such as Linkedin, Tencent, Lenovo, and Baidu have expressed interests to create various sharing platforms where their clients could use to their advantage.

The departure of foreign technology companies such as Google, Adobe and Twitter is not unexpected as the Chinese government now requires technology companies to provide them the secret "source code". With access to the source codes, patented ideas could be stolen easily. Foreign companies have to make the difficult decision of transferring proprietary technologies which will eventually dilute their international competitiveness or miss out on the world fastest growing market.

10

Recent Corporate Events

Case of Yum! Brands

Yum! Brands which owns and manages the KFC and Pizza Hut brands decided to spin-off its China's operation through a public listing. As of November 2016, Yum! China became a master franchisee of Yum! Brands Inc, and is managed by a team of predominantly Chinese executives. Yum! China currently operates approximately 6,900 restaurants in over 1,000 cities. China accounts for half of Yum! Brands' global sales. The company has announced plans to spin off its China operations to create a more focused business.

Yum! China will have two new investors: Private-equity firm Primavera Capital and Alibaba's Ant Financial. The latter is formerly known as Alipay and operates the Alipay payment platform. Ant is also a shareholder in food delivery website Eleme. With the collaboration with Alibaba, Yum! China customers could place orders online and pay with their mobile phones. While the total investment of Primavera Capital and Ant Financial accounted for about 6% of total shares of

Yum! China, the move is, nevertheless, significant after the withdrawal of a consortium backed by China Investment Corp failed to agree on a price with KFC and Pizza Hut.

As a spin-off entity, Yum! China may need to reassess its strategies. It has to relook at the implications of government policies and regulations. At the same time, it has to review the relationships with its distributors, suppliers, and technological partners. The new management will have to improve the brand positioning of Yum! in new regions within China.

Case of McDonald's China

Like Yum!, McDonald's is also looking for strategic partners in China. It is selling a 20-year mass franchise rights in China and Hong Kong which could fetch up to USD2 billion. The company has invited China Cinda Asset Management Co., Beijing Sanyuan Foods, Sanpower Group Co., and Green Tree Hospitality to bid for the franchise rights. Through refranchising, McDonald's plans to have 95 percent of its restaurants in north Asia under local ownership. Unlike Yum!, McDonald's has no plans for a public listing for its China operations. It currently operates more than 2,000 restaurants in China.

McDonald's too needs to adapt to the rise of online shopping. To date, none of the potential suitors are dominant online players like Ant Financial which invested in Yum! China.

Besides China, McDonald's is selling off its operations in Japan where it has almost 3,000 outlets, Taiwan where it operates over 400 stores, and South Korea where it has over 600 restaurants.

McDonald's faces stiff competition from chains like Yum!, Kung Fu, Ajisen and Starbucks. McDonald's needs to reposition itself in the region if it wishes to continue playing a major role in the North Asia.

The above two cases highlight the need for foreign companies to relook at their internationalisation strategies in China. Finding a local partner and having a local team who understands the domestic market are critical success factors for foreign firms operating in China. Both Western and Chinese companies have more to gain from collaboration than from direct competition (Figure 13).

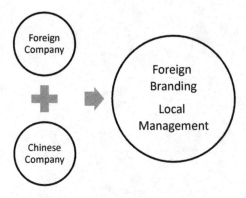

Figure 13: Collaboration Model

Section 3

Chinese Management Styles

Chapter

11

Chinese Management Practices

C hanges in economic environments will require changes in management styles. Modern Chinese management practices tend to embrace both Chinese and Western theories and cultures. Many traditional values continue alongside modern values and shape the thinking of younger Chinese managers. Western approaches are seen as more impersonal and focus on processes and contracts while Chinese managers emphasise more on long-term and social relationships.

Chinese owners normally maintain control of the company and pass the ownership to their sons and daughters. The elder son is the natural heir to the parent's business. As more younger generation of managers are educated overseas or have been exposed to Western influences, they tend to incorporate both Chinese and Western management concepts in their management style (Cao & Li, 2010; Connor *et al.*, 2013). While many Chinese managers are open to adopting new ideas, they still adhere to the traditional values which were formed at an early stage of their life (Jung *et al.*, 2010; Fenby, 2013).

In the West, businesses are driven by a strong regulatory and legal environment. While contracts are also a norm in China, there is also more room for negotiations after the agreement is signed. Chinese managers value interpersonal relationships as a key to successful business dealings while Western managers rely heavily on contracts. Chinese managers see the contract as a beginning to a long-term relationships where future business opportunities warrant both parties to be more flexible in their current agreement. Western managers, on the other hand, may see their Chinese counterparts as untrustworthy when the latter seek to make some amendments to the terms and conditions of the contract.

Chinese leadership style is highly paternalistic with the owner playing the role of patriarch or matriarch and employees as children. The traditional values of familism and patriarchy often extend beyond family boundaries and are applied to vertical authority relationships based on seniority in the organisation (Aycan, 2006). The owner expects employees to be loyal and obedient to him (or her). This paternalistic leadership style is a major hindrance to recruiting new employees as employees are now more demanding and expect to be treated with respect. To reprimand an employee the same way as a father reprimands a son is becoming increasingly intolerable to younger employees. Often the business owners will overrule the decisions of professional managers citing their hierarchy or that they are the pay masters of the professional managers. This inflated ego further aggravates the relationship leading to high turnover of employees. Another setback of paternalism is that it encourages favouritism. Employees who are incompetent are promoted as they gain the favour of the owners while capable employees who often express their opinions which are contradictory to the owners may be shelved aside.

In cultures with a high power distance context, organisations have steep hierarchies with differences in power between individuals and groups (Carl et al., 2004). This wide status differences between a leader and his subordinate is widely accepted as part of the society (Pellegrini & Scandura, 2008).

Paternalistic leadership can be either benevolent or exploitative. In benevolent paternalism, the manager shows care and concern for the employees. Employees, on the other hand, show their loyalty and commitment to the employer. However, many cases of paternalistic leadership tend to be exploitative with the manager placing high demands from employees while providing minimal support and resources. This causes high resentment from employees resulting in low productivity and high turnovers.

Relating closely to paternalism is nepotism. In many Chinese organisations, family relationships with the owners play an important role in the recruitment of senior managers. Trusted family members are put into senior positions of the companies. Often, this leads to the "princelings" syndrome where children of business owners were given high positions and power without much achievements of their own.

Many authors attempt to over emphasise the differences between Chinese and Western management styles. There are no clear distinctions between them as many Chinese managers have incorporated some aspects of Western management practices in their daily activities. At the same time, Western managers have also seen the benefits of adopting some form of Chinese management practices such as harmony and moral values. Rather than emphasising the differences, it will be more meaningful to highlight the common values and beliefs between Eastern and Western cultures as the world economies become increasingly intertwined with each other.

The convergence of Western and Chinese managerial styles has taken place in many Chinese companies. For example, in the case of Alibaba Group, Jack Ma uses Chinese culture as a base while adopting Western managerial theories and principles. Jack Ma's management style and philosophy are widely influenced by Daoism, Confucianism and Buddhism. At the same time, he advocates Western ideas of staff motivation, training and development.

Case of Lenovo

Lenovo Group, likewise, experienced challenges in integrating IBM's corporate culture following its acquisition of the U.S. giant in 2011. Lenovo's chairman, Liu Chuanzhi, adopted the strategy of keeping all IBM sales people to maintain the relationship with its clients.

At the same time, he introduced plans to integrate Chinese and American managers. Lenovo's top management team consists of four Chinese managers and four U.S. managers who work together. The eight senior executives look at the macro picture as well as micro issues when making major decisions. To strengthen the integration, all new recruits are trained in Western concept of teamwork and business methods. The two top IBM executives who had been with Lenovo since its acquisition remained for over 10 years are Thomas Looney and Peter Hortensius. Thomas Looney is the general manager for Lenovo North America while Peter Hortensius is the chief technology officer.

Lenovo also acquired Motorola for USD2.9 billion and IBM's low-end server business for USD2.3 billion to its portfolio in 2014, boosting its position in the hand phone and server markets.

Lenovo was able to successfully integrate IBM's culture with its own culture as it pays particular attention to the needs of various stakeholders (Figure 14).

The company has adopted the business model of producing in low cost centre in China. With the resources generated from production, it has invested in Research and Development to build up its design capabilities.

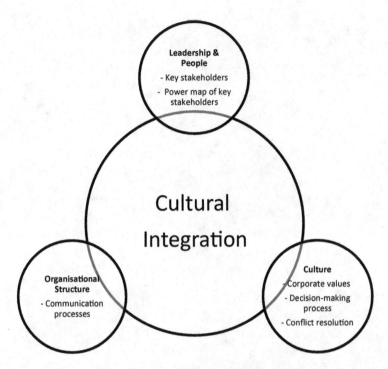

Figure 14: Cultural Integration Framework

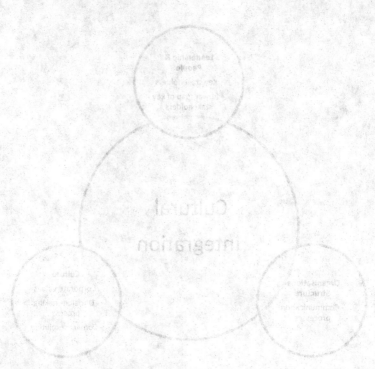

Chapter

12

Guanxi

Based on Hofstede's cultural dimension model, China is high on power distance, uncertainty/avoidance and long term/short term orientation (Hofstede & Bond, 1998). It is low on individualism/collectivism dimension and records higher feministic traits (Chinta & Capar, 2007).

The high power distance figure symbolises a top-down management approach where employees acknowledge the authority of their managers. As businesses in China involve a lot of dealings with the government authorities, managers have to spend a lot of time developing *guanxi* or relationships with officials. While bribery is illegal, the practice is still prevalent in China to get things done readily.

Guanxi involves building trust, commitment, communication and cooperation (Naude & Buttle, 2000). Trust represents confidence (Garbarino & Johnson, 1999) and non-exploitation (Dwyer *et al.*, 1987). It is the key to successful business collaboration. Communication is necessary to minimise conflicts arising between parties to the transaction. It is necessary to build and maintain long-term relationships. Chinese managers value long-term relationships due to their cultural preference for long-term orientation

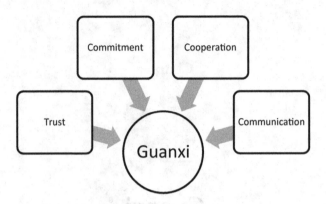

Figure 15: Development of *Guanxi*

(Yen & Barnes, 2011). Figure 15 illustrates the keys to the development of *guanxi*.

Chinese managers avoid making risky decisions. They have to bear in mind that decisions are aimed at promoting group cooperation and maintaining harmony. The close cooperation between business people and government bureaucrats is more obvious in China than in Western countries.

Although the influence of Confucianism is still prevalent, it is slowly diminishing as China enjoys economic growth and as the country becomes more open. Following China's entry into the World Trade Organisation, more foreign companies are investing in China. At the same time, China's enterprises are aggressively expanding overseas or establishing joint ventures with international companies. Such commercial transactions to develop strategic relations with other countries have greatly expanded China's economic influence globally.

Many Chinese managers have incorporated practices from Western countries into their management style. Warner (2010) proposed a hybrid structure for human resources management in China which he called *Confucian HRM*. He noted that maintaining a harmonious social order at work is a traditional Chinese value. At the same time, competency-based selection and performance-based reward systems are gaining popularity in China.

Case of Huawei France

Huawei, China's networking and telecommunications equipment and services giant, established a tech start-up support program called Digital In-Pulse in France in 2014. Recently, its French subsidiary, Huawei France, provided financial and business support to three French technology start-ups. The financial support amounted up to EUR50,000 while the business support included business trips to China and personalised follow-ups from Business France. Through such support, Huawei not only builds *guanxi* with the French authorities but also have access to innovative products and services of the start-ups. To date, nearly 30 French companies have benefited from Huawei France's support. This is a case where a multinational Chinese company is seen supporting smaller foreign companies in its strategy to build goodwill and brand image in the foreign country (Figure 16).

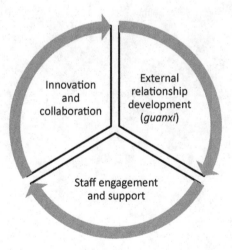

Figure 16: Globalisation of Huawei in France

13

Management Paradox: Divide and Rule

While many Chinese managers advocate Confucius' teachings of maintaining social order and harmony, they are also adopting a divide and rule management style to consolidate their power and position in the organisation. This strategy breaks up groups and prevents alliances from forming. At the same time, the manager also creates rivalries between the groups and foments disagreements between the two groups.

Managers high in dominance motivation desire power. They may use manipulative and coercive ways to achieve and maintain their position. They may try to socially isolate a talented subordinate when they feel threatened (Case, 2014). This is consistent when earlier research which showed that managers low in prestige motivation tended to isolate skilled employees (Fast et al., 2012).

Sun Tzu said:

> "By discovering the enemy's dispositions and remaining invisible ourselves, we can keep our forces concentrated, while the enemy's must be divided.

We can form a single united body, while the enemy must split up into fractions. Hence there will be a whole pitted against separate parts of a whole, which means that we shall be many to the enemy's few."

This concept of Divide and Rule is also prevalent in the West. Niccolo Machiavelli (1469–1527), an Italian politician, identified this application in military strategy. He wrote in his book *Discourses*:

"For the farther the Roman armies went from Rome, the more necessary did such prolongation of the military commands seem to the Senate, and the more frequently did they practise it. Two evils resulted from this: militarization. The first was that fewer men became experienced in the command of armies, and therefore distinguished reputation was confined to a few. The other was that by the general remaining a long while in command of an army, the soldiers became so attached to him personally that they made themselves his partisans, and, forgetful of the Senate, recognized no chief or authority but him. It was thus that Sylla and Marius were enabled to find soldiers willing to follow their lead even against the republic itself. And it was by this means that Cæsar was enabled to make himself absolute master of his country."

Case of Haier's Zhang Ruimin

Zhang Ruimin, Chairman of the Haier Group, seems to be using the divide and rule strategy as part of his transformation exercise of Haier. He has dismantled the traditional corporate structure of Haier and created hundreds of micro-enterprises. As a result, 10,000 middle-level managerial jobs have been eliminated. The relationship between the head office and the newly-formed micro-enterprises is like an investor and an entrepreneur.

With such a flat structure, Zhang Ruimin has essentially consolidated his power as he has broken up the Group into small entities which compete with each other. Many senior executives found that their positions had been lowered. Dissenters who disagreed or unable to adapt to the transformation exercise had left the company, either voluntarily or involuntarily. This downsizing could be a planned elimination of jobs or positions (Kets de Vries and Balazs, 1997) and also reduction of the overall workforce (Cameron *et al.*, 1991).

This transformation exercise creates distrust among members of various teams as they compete to gain more resources from the headquarters. Employees also have to readjust to a new reward system which is based on the revenue they bring into the company. As such, two or more micro-enterprises may be competing for the same client. This may give rise to issues of unethical selling behaviour as an employee's salary is not determined by the headquarters, but by his own performance. Haier also created a policy of *"catfish management"* where there is a shadow manager who will take over as divisional manager if the incumbent divisional manager fails to achieve his target in three months. This further creates distrust among team members within each micro-enterprise.

The new structure will also discourage innovation as research and development is generally regarded as expenses. It will normally take a long period to develop and commercialise a new product. Meanwhile, the managers running the micro-enterprises will face cash flow constraints if they are unable to launch the new products within schedule.

It may still in the early days to determine if the new business model will work for Haier. With so many micro-enterprises within the Group, there is much duplication of activities such as marketing, accounting and administration. Haier is moving away from being a traditional electrical appliance manufacturer to becoming a venture investor. While such a strategy may reduce overall manpower, research and administration costs, the company also stands to lose much valued aspects of a job such as sense of belonging, teamwork, job security and employees' pride working for a familiar name. Insecure employees are less inclined to remain with the organisation (Hartley *et al.*, 1991).

Section 4

Sun Tzu Art of Management

Sun Tzu Art of Modern Management

I n addition to the influences of Confucianism, Daoism, and Buddhism, China's business culture is also influenced by Sun Tzu, an ancient military strategist.

The *Art of War* is an ancient military treatise written by Sun Tzu around 500 B.C. It consists of 13 chapters, with each one focusing on different aspects of military strategies and tactics. Many business people have applied the principles of the *Art of War* into their management strategies.

Sun Tzu's classical strategies provide a guide for understanding and reacting to the changing competitive business environment. Business owners need to position their companies accordingly in response to their competitors' strengths and benchmark their performance versus their competitors. Business leaders could apply Sun Tzu's Six Principles in their daily business practices (Figure 17):

1) Capture your market share without destroying it;
2) Avoid competitors strength and attack their weakness;

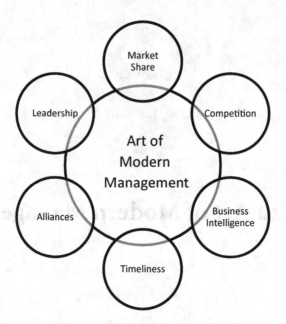

Figure 17: Art of Modern Management

3) Maximise the power of business intelligence;
4) Use speed to overcome the competition;
5) Build alliances and strategic control points to your advantage;
6) Develop your leadership skills to maximise potential of your employees.

Table 1 lists the 13 chapters of Sun Tzu Art of War.

In the following chapters, the author highlights the important concepts of each chapter from the *Art of War* which are relevant to today's business environment.

Table 1: Sun Tzu Art of War

Chapter	Strategy
1	Analysis and Laying Plans
2	Waging War
3	Attack by Stratagem
4	Tactical Dispositions
5	Use of Energy
6	Weakness and Strength
7	Military Combat
8	Variation of Tactics
9	Army on the March
10	Classification of Terrain
11	Nine Terrains
12	Fiery Attack
13	Employing Spies

Chapter

15

Analysis and Laying Plans

Sun Tzu said:

"The art of war is of vital importance to the State. It is a matter of life and death, a road either to safety or to ruin. Hence it is a subject of inquiry which can on no account be neglected. The art of war, then, is governed by five constant factors, to be taken into account in one's deliberations, when seeking to determine the conditions obtaining in the field. These are: (1) The Moral Law; (2) Heaven; (3) Earth; (4) The Commander; (5) Doctrine.

The Moral Law causes the people to be in complete accord with their ruler, so that they will follow him regardless of their lives, undismayed by any danger. Heaven signifies night and day, cold and heat, times and seasons. Earth comprises distances, great and small; danger and security; open ground and narrow passes; the chances of life and death. The Commander stands for the virtues of wisdom, sincerity, benevolence, courage and strictness.

Now the general who wins a battle makes many calculations in his temple ere the battle is fought. The general who loses a battle makes but few *calculations beforehand. Thus do many calculations lead to victory, and few calculations to defeat: how much more no calculation at all! It is by attention to this point that I can foresee who is likely to win or lose."*

Business Applications

Applying Sun Tzu's strategies to the modern business environment, we could equate the five constant factors shown in Figure 18.

1) Moral = Commitment;
2) Heaven = Competition;
3) Earth = 5Ps (Place, Promotion, Price, Product, People);
4) Commander = Leadership;
5) Doctrine = Guiding Principles.

A good leader possesses the following attributes:

1) Committing to the growth and development of the organisation and its employees;
2) Being honest and open and showing respect for all employees;
3) Showing stewardship qualities, guiding the organisation through the changing business environment;
4) Setting high ethical standards and maintaining good corporate governance in the organisation.

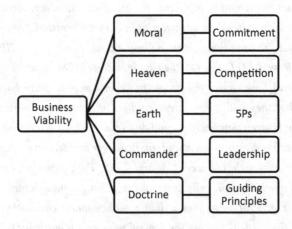

Figure 18: Business Viability

Sun Tzu quoted:

> *"When one treats people with benevolence, justice and righteousness, and reposes confidence in them, the army will be united in mind and all will be happy to serve their leaders."*

A good business leader possesses strategic planning capabilities. This is partly illustrated by the 5Ps framework (Figure 19).

The 5Ps are key marketing elements which help a manager thinks about how he can add value and differentiate the company's products and services from its competitors.

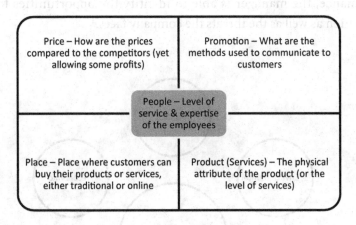

Figure 19: 5Ps of Marketing

Sun Tzu's first chapter states that:

> *"Now the general who wins a battle makes many calculations in his temple before the battle is fought."*

Applying this concept to modern management technique, a manager needs to conduct an environmental analysis to assess the level of threats and opportunities that may affect the organisation's performance. Two commonly used strategic analysis tools are PESTLE and PORTER's FIVE FORCES.

Incorporating PESTLE

The letters in PESTLE denote the following factors (Figure 20):

P = Political Factors
E = Economic Factors
S = Social Factors
T = Technological Factors
L = Legal Factors
E = Environmental Factors

With a detailed analysis of the various factors impacting a company's performance, the manager is able to identify the opportunities for the organisation as well as the threats the company faces.

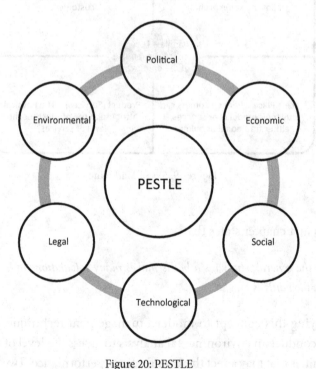

Figure 20: PESTLE

Incorporating Porter's Five Forces

Porter's five forces is a useful tool to assist the manager to understand both the strength of the company's competitive position and the strength of the position it considers moving into. There are five forces that determine competitive power in a business situation (Figure 21). These are:

1) Supplier Power;
2) Buyer Power;
3) Competitive Rivalry;
4) Threat of Substitution;
5) Threat of New Entry.

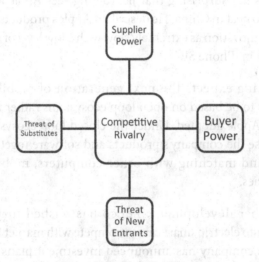

Figure 21: Porter's Five Forces

Case of LeEco

LeEco is often compared to Netflix of United States. The company's businesses include video and content streaming, smart televisions, mobile phones, and more recently smart supercars.

The company aims to be the top five smartphone makers in China after its latest investment of HKD1.05 billion in another smartphone company, Coolpad Group. LeEco holds 28.9% in Coolpad and Jia Yueting, the founder of LeEco, has been appointed the new Chairman of Coolpad. The two companies expect to sell more than 50 million smartphones in 2016 under a dual-brand strategy.

Coolpad phones are sold through mobile operators while LeEco phones are sold directly to customers. The former phones are considered medium-level smartphones while the latter phones are priced at premium levels. In 2015, Coolpad sold over 30 million phones in China as compared to LeEco 10 million. Under the dual brand strategy, LeEco will assist Coolpad to shift to the internet business model.

It is thus not surprising that Jia Yueting sees Apple as the main competitor to beat in China. He described Apple's products as obsolete and that its innovation as extremely slow with a low level of technology, as evidenced in iPhone SE.

Jia Yueting expects the next generation of mobile internet technologies to be based on open loop ecosystems rather than closed loop which Apple adopted. Under the closed loop ecosystem, Apple customers use the company's products and software together instead of mixing and matching with other computers, mobile devices and accessories.

In another development, LeEco has pushed forward with investment into electric smart cars to compete with market leader Tesla Motors. The company has announced investment plans of RMB12 billion in an electric car factory in eastern China, with an estimated production output of 400,000 cars by 2018. To strengthen its entry into the automobile market, LeEco is teaming up with British car marker Aston Martin.

LeEco is not the only one who is interested in entering the electric car business. Internet giant Tencent Holdings is partnering Taiwan's Hon Hai Precision Industry and China's Harmony Auto to develop electric cars. At the same time, Baidu Holdings has also announced plans to develop driverless cars to rival Google, Tesla, General Motors, and Ford's entry into the autonomous car market.

While Jia Yueting sees opportunities for hand phones and smart cars, he is also constrained by limitations of financial and human resources (Figure 22). In addition, he faces stiff competition from major hand phone producers such as Apple, Samsung, and Xiaomi. The electric smart car market faces some technological challenges as evidenced from the recent fatal accident of a Tesla car in the United States.

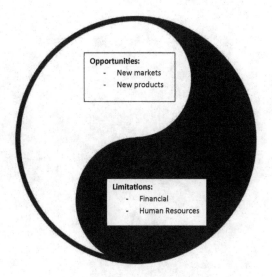

Figure 22: Balancing Constraints with Opportunities

Chapter

16

Waging War

S

un Tzu said:

"In the operations of war, where there are in the field a thousand swift chariots, as many heavy chariots, and a hundred thousand mail-clad soldiers, with provisions enough to carry them a thousand li, the expenditure at home and at the front, including entertainment of guests, small items such as glue and paint, and sums spent on chariots and armour, will reach the total of a thousand ounces of silver per day. Such is the cost of raising an army of 100,000 men.

When you engage in actual fighting, if victory is long in coming, then men's weapons will grow dull and their ardour will be damped. If you lay siege to a town, you will exhaust your strength.

Again, if the campaign is protracted, the resources of the State will not be equal to the strain. Now, when your weapons are dulled, your ardour damped, your strength exhausted and your treasure spent, other chieftains will spring up to take advantage of your extremity. Then no man, however wise, will be able to avert the consequences that must ensue."

Case of JD.com

JD.com is China's second largest B2C online platform. The company recently announced it is gearing up its virtual reality (VR) and augmented reality (AR) technologies on its online shopping platform. This will place it on a head-on competition with Alibaba Group which had recently invested in mixed reality start-up Magic Leap. Alibaba also announced that it is setting up a virtual reality lab, GnomeMagic Lab.

The new VR and AR technologies will help enhance shoppers' experience by allowing customers to see virtual items in a real environment. JD.com also disclosed that it has signed agreement with VR manufacturer, Beijing Baofeng Mojing Technology, to sell 15 million VR headsets over the next three years.

In another development, JD.com also revealed plans to invest USD700 million for a 10 percent stake in supermarket chain Yonghui Superstores. The company plans to combine its online channels with the latter's 364 traditional supermarkets.

The online-to-offline (O2O) retail services segment has seen several activities lately. Another major supermarket chain, Renrenle, plans to raise RMB2.3 billion for an e-commerce platform called Renren Legou.

While many companies are investing aggressively on O2O to position themselves as the dominant players in China's retailing sector, smaller players may not have the financial capability to compete with giants such as Tencent, Baidu, and Alibaba.

Business Applications

Applying Sun Tzu's strategies to the business environment, companies need to have the proper organisational structures, resources, and detailed marketing plans if they desire to gain new market shares (Figure 23).

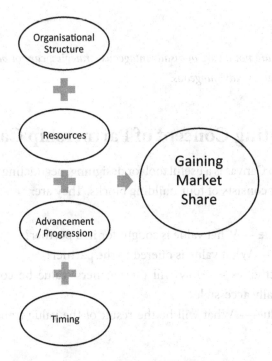

Figure 23: Gaining Market Share

Success in business could only be achieved through proper planning. A head-on campaign against a competitor can incur high costs and resources. The company needs to do a detailed analysis of its organisational structure as well as the available resources. The timing on when to proceed with a project or plan is important if the company wishes to secure maximum benefits from the venture. A prolonged campaign against a competitor will easily drain out human and financial resources.

This chapter is critical to understanding why Sun Tzu advocated "winning without conflict". Modern-day managers should look at strategies which result in a win-win situation for all parties. These could include building partnerships, alliances, product differentiation and geographical segregation.

Sun Tzu noted:

> *"Those who are not aware of disadvantageous strategies, cannot be aware of strategies that are advantageous."*

Incorporating Concept of Partnership Canvas

The Partnership Canvas is a useful tool for designing, negotiating and adapting partnerships. It consists of four building blocks. They are:

1) Desired Value — What value is sought for in a partner?
2) Value Offer — What value is offered to the partner?
3) Transfer Activities — How will the partners' value be connected and made mutually accessible?
4) Created Value — What will be the result of the value transfer between partners?

Through visual presentation, a manager will be able to develop a more collaborative rather than a competitive business environment. Figure 24 shows the building blocks of the Partnership Canvas.

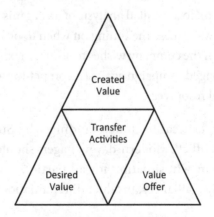

Figure 24: Partnership Canvas

Case of Geely Holdings

Founded in 1986 as a refrigerator maker, Geely Holdings is now an international automotive manufacturing company with over 900 retail outlets. The company is headed by Li Shufu, a Masters of Science graduate from Yanshan University.

In 2013, Geely acquired London Taxi Company which operates London's black taxi. London Taxi Company, founded in 1899, went bankrupt three years ago. But, thanks to Geely, the company was given a new lease of life. Geely plans to build a GBP250 million manufacturing facility for London Taxi Company near Coventry which will begin production this year (2017). Through the investment in a bankrupt company, Geely is seen as a white knight. Its investment in the plant will also create jobs for the U.K. employees. Through the acquisition, Geely has managed to secure an iconic British brand. The company also acquired Volvo Cars from Ford Motors in 2010 for USD1.3 billion.

Geely recruited Peter Horbury as its chief car designer. Peter Horbury was the chief designer for Volvo in the 1990s. He also oversaw Volvo, Jaguar, Aston Martin and Ford brands from 2002. Peter aims to give Geely's car an upmarket image through new designs and rebranding.

Geely aims to move its products range from the low end to the middle end for its own brands. It has added the *Emgrand* brand to complement the lower end brand. With Volvo, the company now has a high end brand (Figure 25).

Geely has established three Volvo factories since the acquisition. It currently employs 5,000 workers and boasts a dealer strength of 200. Despite the successful turnaround of Volvo, Geely has not fully integrated Volvo into the Group. It has a lot to learn from Volvo in becoming a global brand.

Volvo and Geely have different cultures. Volvo has a more bureaucratic structure while Geely has a more entrepreneurial structure. The other reason full integration is not possible is the language barrier as Volvo staff speak mainly Swedish although they are conversant in English. On the other hand, few Geely employees speak good English (Figure 26).

The surge in demand for smaller cars and the impending expiration of sales tax cut in China have boosted car sales for the first eight months of 2016. Total vehicle sales jumped by 12.8 percent to 14.4 million. With Volvo in its portfolio, Geely is set on its path to becoming a more aggressive player in the automotive industry.

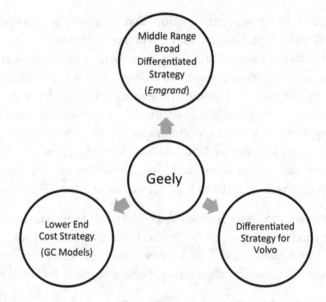

Figure 25: Geely's Differentiation Strategies

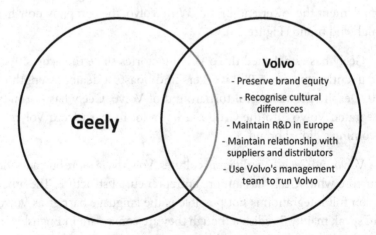

Figure 26: Geely's Approach to Volvo

Chapter

Attack by Stratagem

S un Tzu said:

"In the practical art of war, the best thing of all is to take the enemy's country whole and intact; to shatter and destroy it is not so good. So, too, it is better to recapture an army entire than to destroy it, to capture a regiment, a detachment or a company entire than to destroy them. Hence to fight and conquer in all your battles is not supreme excellence; supreme excellence consists in breaking the enemy's resistance without fighting.

Thus the highest form of generalship is to balk the enemy's plans; the next best is to prevent the junction of the enemy's forces; the next in order is to attack the enemy's army in the field; and the worst policy of all is to besiege walled cities.

Thus we may know that there are five essentials for victory: (1) He will win who knows when to fight and when not to fight. (2) He will win who knows how to handle both superior and inferior forces. (3) He will win whose army is animated by the same spirit throughout all its ranks. (4) He will win who, prepared himself, waits to take the enemy unprepared. (5) He will win who has military capacity and is not interfered with by the sovereign. Hence the saying: If you know the enemy and know yourself, you need not fear the result of a hundred battles. If you know yourself but not the enemy, for every victory gained you will also suffer a defeat. If you know neither the enemy nor yourself, you will succumb in every battle."

Business Applications

This chapter covers market penetration strategies. Sun Tzu advises expansion of market share in order to survive. Businesses not only have to defend their existing markets, but also seek new markets.

The company has to first secure its market position by identifying its strengths and unique selling points. Next, it has to determine its market positioning. Thirdly, it has to do a careful analysis of the environment conditions before deciding on any major campaign. The process of environmental analysis has been described in Chapter 1: Analysis and Laying Plans.

Figure 27 illustrates the market positioning process using Sun Tzu's ideas.

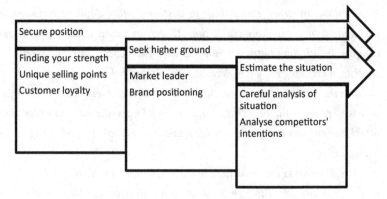

Figure 27: Market Positioning

Incorporating Concept of Ansoff Matrix

Ansoff Matrix is a strategic planning tool that links a company's marketing strategy with its general strategic direction. It presents four alternative growth strategies in the form of a 2 × 2 matrix. One dimension of the matrix considers "products" and the other dimension considers "markets" (Table 2).

Table 2: Ansoff Matrix

		Products	
		Existing	New
Markets	Existing	Market Penetration	Product Development
	New	Market Development	Diversification

The matrix offers a framework to assess strategies for growth. Managers have to decide if they wish to adopt one of the four strategies.

1) Market Penetration — Increasing existing market share
2) Market Development — Developing new markets for existing products or services
3) Product Development — Developing new products or services for existing markets
4) Diversification — Developing new products or services for new markets

Sun Tzu said:

"Know the other and know yourself, fight one hundred battles without danger. Know not the other and yet know yourself, one victory for one defeat. Know not the other and know not yourself, every fight is certain defeat."

Case of South China Morning Post

South China Morning Post, a 112-year-old company, was recently sold by the Kuok Group of Hong Kong to e-commerce giant, Alibaba Group, for HKD2.06 billion (USD266 million). The company has faced stiff competition from free online newspapers. Revenue from foreign advertisers has also been reduced significantly in recent years. As part of the Alibaba Group, the company is able to leverage on the diverse network of its new owner and gain easier access to mainland advertisers. The newspaper company has also impose self-censorship on stories that it thinks is politically critical of the Chinese government.

For Alibaba, the purchase of South China Morning Post fits into its overall strategy of investing in media assets. The acquisition of the newspaper company will enable it to have greater access to international readers as it is a favourite newspaper for reporting on China. The Group has also invested in financial news network China Business Network and online video company Youku Tudou, Inc.

18

Tactical Dispositions

S un Tzu said:

"The good fighters of old first put themselves beyond the possibility of defeat, and then waited for an opportunity of defeating the enemy. To secure ourselves against defeat lies in our own hands, but the opportunity of defeating the enemy is provided by the enemy himself. Thus the good fighter is able to secure himself against defeat, but cannot make certain of defeating the enemy. Hence the saying: One may know how to conquer without being able to do it. Security against defeat implies defensive tactics; ability to defeat the enemy means taking the offensive.

Standing on the defensive indicates insufficient strength; attacking, a superabundance of strength. The general who is skilled in defense hides in the most secret recesses of the earth; he who is skilled in attack flashes forth from the topmost heights of heaven. Thus on the one hand we have ability to protect ourselves; on the other, a victory that is complete. The consummate leader cultivates the moral law, and strictly adheres to method and discipline; thus it is in his power to control success.

In respect of military method, we have, firstly, Measurement; secondly, Estimation of quantity; thirdly, Calculation; fourthly, Balancing of chances; fifthly, Victory. Measurement owes its existence to Earth; Estimation of quantity to Measurement; Calculation to Estimation of quantity; Balancing of chances to Calculation; and Victory to Balancing of chances."

Business Applications

In tactical dispositions, two companies seek to discover each other's strategies, strengths and weaknesses. It is essential for companies to conceal their financial resources or marketing budgets in promotional campaigns. Companies have to assess their own competitive positions and defend their existing market share. At the same time, they have to seek opportunities to expand their market share, either locally or internationally (Figure 28).

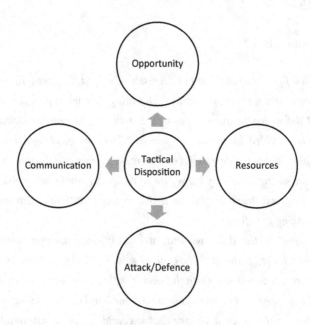

Figure 28: Tactical Disposition

Positioning Map

The Positioning Map is a perceptual tool which assists the company to analyse the position or perception of the company's products and services, in respect of two specific characteristics. The two product characteristics are *Price* along the Y-axis and *Quality* along the X-axis.

With the Positioning Map, companies are able to classify their existing market products or services in relation to their competitors (Figure 29).

Figure 29: Positioning Map

Sun Tzu said:

"With skillful positioning, defeat or victory is apparent to everyone well in advance of any confrontation. Those who are skilled in conflict establish a situation that cannot be defeated."

Case of Alipay Wallet and WeChatPay

China's mobile payment market is expected to hit USD5 trillion by 2019. The two largest players in China's mobile payment market are Alipay Wallet and Tencent's WeChatPay. Alipay, launched in 2004, was initially developed to facilitate online shopping and trading for its Taobao and Tmall platforms. The service has since expanded to include Alibaba Music, Alibaba Pictures, Alibaba Sports and Youku. Alipay is estimated to have 50 percent market share of the mobile payment market in China.

WeChatPay, launched in 2013, grew from Tencent's QQ and Tencent Games. It is now both a payment platform as well as an instant messaging service. Users can pay in stores, on websites and third party applications. Through the use of social media and instant messaging service, WeChat has opened up new opportunities for retailers to interact with their customers. The company's market share in China is estimated to be 10.6 percent.

The battle is still ongoing. With China being the largest online market, perhaps there is enough room for both players. Innovation is the key to maintaining their market share for mobile online payment.

19

Use of Energy

S un Tzu said:

"The control of a large force is the same principle as the control of a few men: it is merely a question of dividing up their numbers. Fighting with a large army under your command is nowise different from fighting with a small one: it is merely a question of instituting signs and signals. To ensure that your whole host may withstand the brunt of the enemy's attack and remain unshaken — this is effected by maneuvers direct and indirect.

That the impact of your army may be like a grindstone dashed against an egg — this is effected by the science of weak points and strong. In all fighting, the direct method may be used for joining battle, but indirect methods will be needed in order to secure victory. Indirect tactics, efficiently applied, are inexhaustible as Heaven and Earth, unending as the flow of rivers and streams; like the sun and moon, they end but to begin anew; like the four seasons, they pass away to return once more.

The clever combatant looks to the effect of combined energy, and does not require too much from individuals. Hence his ability to pick out the right men and utilize combined energy.

When he utilizes combined energy, his fighting men become as it were like unto rolling logs or stones. For it is the nature of a log or stone to remain motionless on level ground, and to move when on a slope; if four-cornered, to come to a standstill, but if round-shaped, to go rolling down. Thus the energy developed by good fighting men is as the momentum of a round stone rolled down a mountain thousands of feet in height."

Business Applications

Sun Tzu advocated fostering a culture of innovation and pushing boundaries. Breaking down boundaries enables businesses to enter new grounds. At the same time, companies need to innovate to stay relevant. Developing a culture of innovation involves garnering the support and commitment of all employees in the organisation (Figure 30).

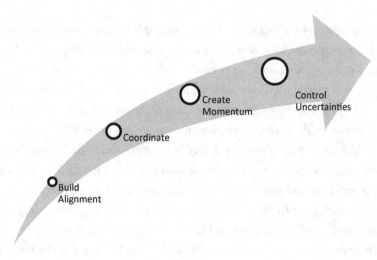

Figure 30: Pushing Boundaries

Business Process Reengineering

Business Process Reengineering (BPR) involves the analysis and redesigning of core business processes to achieve dramatic improvements in productivity. Companies begin their BPR process by adopting a new value system that emphasises customers' needs (Figure 31).

The BPR exercise may impact the entire technological, human and organisational dimensions. Organisational layers and unproductive processes are eliminated in the BPR process. Employees may be reassigned to different duties as a result of the elimination of their tasks. Managers have to learn to deal with the resistance from employees as many would see BPR as an excuse to retrench them. Handled well, the result of a BPR process could be a leaner, meaner and more productive organisation.

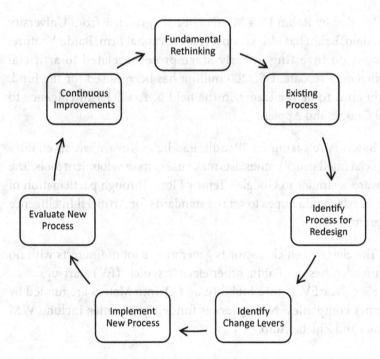

Figure 31: Business Process Reengineering

Sun Tzu noted:

"An army may be likened to water, for just as flowing water avoids the heights and hastens to the lowlands, so an army avoids strength and strikes weakness."

Case of Baidu

China's technology companies are collaborating with their Western counterparts in developing highly sophisticated products. Internet giant Baidu recently unveiled plans to develop driverless vehicles in a partnership with U.S. chipmaker Nvidia Corporation. The project known as "Baidu Brain" simulates the human brain with computer technology. Baidu has already set up a research and development team in Silicon Valley to develop autonomous driving technologies.

Headed by Robin Li, a Masters of Arts graduate from University of Buffalo, Baidu has also set up a venture capital firm, Baidu Venture, to focus on investing in early-stage projects related to artificial intelligence. To date, USD200 million has been raised for the fund. Baidu aims to be the leader in the field of Artificial Intelligence to rival Google and Apple.

Baidu is releasing its "Paddle Paddle" software which enables Artificial Intelligence enthusiasts make use of its development tools. The software is similar to Google's Tensor Flow. Through participation of enthusiasts, Baidu hopes to set the standards for Artificial Intelligence programming.

The electric vehicle sector is generating a lot of interests with no clear leader. Besides Baidu, other electric vehicle (EV) start-ups such as LeSee, NextEV, Future Mobility, and Qiantu Motors are funded by internet companies. Non-internet funded companies include WM Motors and Zhiche Auto.

Case of Haier

Haier is one of the largest makers of electrical goods with sales of over RMB48.8 billion last year. Its CEO, Zhang Ruimin, is a visionary leader who endorses the integration of Western management concepts with traditional Chinese culture. He has broken down the basic building blocks of an organisation by reinventing Haier as a set of open entrepreneurial platforms served by micro-enterprises. The company has been reconfigured into 180 micro-enterprises, each accounting for its own profit and loss. This structure is analogous to a venture incubator which invests in various enterprises.

Haier's 20 platforms include various ecosystems such as *diet ecosystem* for smart fridges, *atmosphere ecosystem* for air conditioners and Goodaymart Logistics. The micro-enterprises compete to design, build and distribute products and also vie for staff and funding from Haier. Zhang Ruimin believes that this business model increases value to all stakeholders. This new approach to research and development is known as "*open innovation*".

To support the *open innovation* strategy, Haier launched HOPE (Haier Open Partnership Ecosystem). At the core of HOPE is an online portal for technological exchange and innovation. New product ideas, research questions and solutions could all be exchanged through the HOPE platform.

Haier shares both risk and rewards with the micro-enterprises. In cases where the project costs exceed the micro-enterprises financial capabilities, they could request for additional funding from Haier. This relatively flat structure gives Haier faster access to new technologies from its partners.

Two other Chinese conglomerates which have adopted the *open innovation* model are Lenovo and Xiaomi.

In the case of Lenovo, the company has set up the New Business Development (NDP) online platform aimed at start-ups in China. Lenovo's partners could use the company's hardware, software and sales channel. It is also planning to expand such collaborations to companies outside of China.

In Xiaomi's case, the company involved its customers in co-designing its products. It invited its customers to provide feedback on its "Miui" Android operating system. Miui allows users to invent new features for the Xiaomi phones. Interacting with customers is one strategy to keep research and development costs low and at the same time gain customers' interest in the company's products. Xiaomi's new business model proves so successful that it counts among its investors Singapore sovereign wealth fund Temasek Holdings, Qualcomm and Russian wealth manager Yuri Milner.

The cases of Haier, Lenovo and Xiaomi illustrate the degree of sophistication of management thinking of Chinese business leaders today. The concept of *Ying* and *Yang* can be adapted in all the above cases. Specifically, top management has looked and answered the following questions for their growth strategies (Figure 32):

1) Managing weakness with strength in leadership;
2) Expanding the business while reducing costs;
3) Empowering employees while holding them accountable;
4) Achieving long-term innovation through short-term results;
5) Becoming a global company while addressing local needs;
6) Opening to new opportunities while strengthening the core businesses.

Figure 32: Growth Strategies

20

Weakness and Strength

S un Tzu said:

> "Whoever is first in the field and awaits the coming of the enemy, will be fresh for the fight; whoever is second in the field and has to hasten to battle will arrive exhausted. Therefore the clever combatant imposes his will on the enemy, but does not allow the enemy's will to be imposed on him. By holding out advantages to him, he can cause the enemy to approach of his own accord; or, by inflicting damage, he can make it impossible for the enemy to draw near.
>
> If the enemy is taking his ease, he can harass him; if well supplied with food, he can starve him out; if quietly encamped, he can force him to move. Appear at points which the enemy must hasten to defend; march swiftly to places where you are not expected. An army may march great distances without distress, if it marches through country where the enemy is not. You can be sure of succeeding in your attacks if you only attack places which are undefended. You can ensure the safety of your defense if you only hold positions that cannot be attacked.

> *Hence that general is skillful in attack whose opponent does not know what to defend; and he is skillful in defense whose opponent does not know what to attack."*

Business Applications

The business environment is full of uncertainties. Companies do not fully reveal their strengths and weaknesses. They attempt to conceal their weaknesses for obvious commercial reasons. These could include portraying an image of financial viability to their banks or investors, product quality to their customers, and organisational stability to their employees. Managers have to distinguish the difference between reality and illusion in their companies and also that of their competitors. They have to seek out pockets of opportunities in the marketplace and find a niche for their products or services. Many managers tend to be overly optimistic of their companies' own marketing programmes and over-evaluate the performance of their brands. At the same time, they tend to under-evaluate the performances of major competitors (Weber, 2001).

Figure 33 illustrates the Strengths and Weaknesses of an organisation. Companies have to be aware of the differences between real weakness and perceived weakness of competitors before they embark on any competitive strategies.

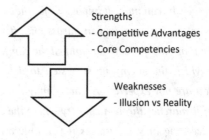

Strengths
- Competitive Advantages
- Core Competencies

Weaknesses
- Illusion vs Reality

Figure 33: Strengths and Weaknesses

Sun Tzu quoted:

"Water shapes its course according to the nature of the ground over which it flows."

Water flows between the gaps of rocks and crevices. Similarly, businesses are able to find opportunities if they conduct a detailed analysis of the various environmental factors affecting their business.

SWOT Analysis

SWOT is the acronym for Strengths, Weaknesses, Opportunities and Threats (Figure 34). It is a tool to help businesses craft out a strategy to distinguish themselves from their competitors. Strengths and Weaknesses are internal to the organisation while Opportunities and Threats relate to external factors.

Internal factors include the following:

1) Financial Resources;
2) Physical Resources;
3) Human Resources;
4) Trademarks, Patents, Copyrights.

External Resources refer to factors which the company may have no control over. They include:

1) Economic Trends;
2) Market Trends;
3) Demographic Trends;
4) Government Policies.

Sun Tzu quoted:

"Know the enemy and know yourself; in a hundred battles you will never be in peril."

Figure 34: SWOT

Case of Alibaba and Lazada Group

Alibaba plans to invest up to USD1 billion in Singapore e-commerce platform Lazada Group SA. It is negotiating to buy shares from Lazada's existing shareholders, including the United Kingdom's Tesco Plc and Germany's Rocket Internet SE. The Chinese internet growth is slowing down and Alibaba is expanding its coverage in South East Asia through this acquisition.

Alibaba also owns a 14.5 percent stake in Singapore Post. It first acquired a 10 percent stake in Singapore Post for SGD249 million in 2014. The following year, it increased its holding by investing another SGD187 million. It has also agreed to acquire a 34 percent stake in Singapore Post logistic unit, Quantum Solutions International, for SGD92 million. The acquisition will help expand Alibaba's e-commerce infrastructure across the Asia-Pacific region.

Chapter

21

Military Combat

Sun Tzu said:

"In war, the general receives his commands from the sovereign. Having collected an army and concentrated his forces, he must blend and harmonize the different elements thereof before pitching his camp. After that, comes tactical maneuvering, than which there is nothing more difficult. The difficulty of tactical maneuvering consists in turning the devious into the direct, and misfortune into gain. Thus, to take a long and circuitous route, after enticing the enemy out of the way, and though starting after him, to contrive to reach the goal before him, shows knowledge of the artifice of deviation.

Maneuvering with an army is advantageous; with an undisciplined multitude, most dangerous. If you set a fully equipped army in march in order to snatch an advantage, the chances are that you will be too late. On the other hand, to detach a flying column for the purpose involves the sacrifice of its baggage and stores. Thus, if you order your men to roll up their buff-coats, and make forced marches without halting day or night, covering double the usual distance at a stretch, doing a hundred li *in order to wrest an advantage, the leaders of all your three divisions will fall into the hands of the enemy.*

We cannot enter into alliances until we are acquainted with the designs of our neighbours. We are not fit to lead an army on the march unless we are familiar with the face of the country — its mountains and forests, its pitfalls and precipices, its marshes and swamps. We shall be unable to turn natural advantage to account unless we make use of local guides. In war, practice dissimulation, and you will succeed. Whether to concentrate or to divide your troops, must be decided by circumstances."

Business Applications

Companies are able to gain competitive advantage if they manage to control strategically valuable resources. These resources could be physical assets (building, land, natural resources, forest concessions, etc), intangible assets (brands, patents, trademarks, etc), or capabilities (manufacturing processes, business relationships, etc).

Many companies are able to achieve competitive advantage by leveraging on their supply chains. A well-developed supply chain integrates all participants and creates value to the company. Value creation requires collaborative relationships with customers, suppliers and other stakeholders. The management of the company has to be committed to continuous improvements and adapt to changes in the marketplace.

Strategically valuable resources are difficult to copy. However, companies should guard against the dilution of these resources, particularly intangible resources and capabilities. Competitors are constantly investing in new technologies, developing new brands and recruiting capable employees to further expand their market share.

Capturing a dominant market share involves careful planning of resources, having good local knowledge and understanding the competitors' intentions. Companies could increase their market share through innovation such as selling their products online, strengthening customers' loyalty, hiring competitors' employees, and even acquiring competitors' businesses.

Creating strategic alliances with a larger company also enable smaller businesses to negotiate for better deals from suppliers. They could also leverage on the marketing and distribution networks of the larger companies. Through strategic alliances, a company can limit the actions of its competitors and take control of the situation away from its competitors. Figure 35 illustrates the various considerations when dealing with share.

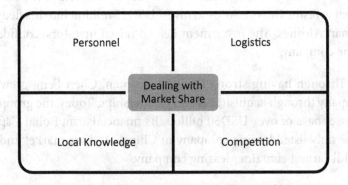

Figure 35: Dealing with Market Share

Sun Tzu said:

"Therefore, those skilled in war bring the enemy to the field of battle and are not brought there by him."

Likewise, effective managers are able to allocate resources well when faced with challenges from competitors.

Case of HNA Group

HNA Group is a diversified conglomerate with interests in aviation, tourism, logistics and eco technology. The company currently operates 1,250 aircrafts and flies to over 200 cities worldwide. Among the airlines it operates and manages are Hainan Airlines, Tianjin Airlines, Deer Jet, Lucky Air, Capital Air, West Air, Fuzhou Airlines, Urumqi Air, Yangtze Air, Guilin Airlines, Africa World Airlines and Aigle Azur.

The company's founder, Chen Feng, is a devout Buddhist who lives a simple life. He claimed that he "doesn't drink, smoke, have banquets, go to karaoke or get massages."

Chen Feng got his big break in 1995 when he managed to persuade global investor George Soros to invest USD25 million into his fledging Hainan Airlines. The investment helped raised investors' confidence in the company.

Through having strong business acumen, Chen Feng grew the company through acquisitions and partnerships. Today, the group has an asset base of over USD50 billion. Its financial arm, Bohai Capital, is the only listed leasing company in China's A-share market and the world's largest container leasing company.

Chen Feng believes that China needs world-class companies to propel the country's growth and influence, both locally and internationally. One main growth strategy is the listing of member companies on stock exchanges. The proposed listing of Hong Kong Airlines, the second largest carrier in Hong Kong, is one such move. While the company has abandoned the public listing plans of Hong Kong Airlines due to the turmoil in China's market in 2015, there is a possibility that it will reactivate the plan again once the market conditions improve.

22

Variation of Tactics

S un Tzu said:

"In war, the general receives his commands from the sovereign, collects his army and concentrates his forces. When in difficult country, do not encamp. In country where high roads intersect, join hands with your allies. Do not linger in dangerously isolated positions. In hemmed-in situations, you must resort to stratagem. In desperate position, you must fight. There are roads which must not be followed, armies which must be not attacked, towns which must be besieged, positions which must not be contested, commands of the sovereign which must not be obeyed.

The general who thoroughly understands the advantages that accompany variation of tactics knows how to handle his troops. The general who does not understand these, may be well acquainted with the configuration of the country, yet he will not be able to turn his knowledge to practical account. So, the student of war who is unversed in the art of war of varying his plans, even though he be acquainted with the Five Advantages, will fail to make the best use of his men.

Hence in the wise leader's plans, considerations of advantage and of disadvantage will be blended together. If our expectation of advantage be tempered in this way, we may succeed in accomplishing the essential part of our schemes. If, on the other hand, in the midst of difficulties we are always ready to seize an advantage, we may extricate ourselves from misfortune.

Reduce the hostile chiefs by inflicting damage on them; and make trouble for them, and keep them constantly engaged; hold out specious allurements, and make them rush to any given point. The art of war teaches us to rely not on the likelihood of the enemy's not coming, but on our own readiness to receive him; not on the chance of his not attacking, but rather on the fact that we have made our position unassailable. There are five dangerous faults which may affect a general: (1) Recklessness, which leads to destruction; (2) cowardice, which leads to capture; (3) a hasty temper, which can be provoked by insults; (4) a delicacy of honour which is sensitive to shame; (5) over-solicitude for his men, which exposes him to worry and trouble."

Business Applications

A common failure of many Chinese managers is the reluctance to accept alternative opinions. They are self-opinionated and often let their ego overtake their sense of reasoning. They tend to micromanage rather than look at the bigger picture as they do not fully agree that their subordinates could do the task well. They feel better when they are constantly directing their employees as this gives them a sense of control over their employees. But, deep down, this kind of actions normally reveals emotional insecurity on their part (Figure 36).

Webster *et al.* (2011) had identified that potential leadership derailers like ego-centredness and micromanaging behaviours have high correlations to measures of self-management: emotional control, desire to impress and stress tolerance.

Rather than micromanaging their employees, Chinese bosses should empower their employees to take up more responsibilities. Through empowerment, employees can become more motivated. Satisfied employees tend to be more committed to their jobs and are more productive (Rue & Byars, 2003). At the same time, the bosses could focus on larger strategic planning processes.

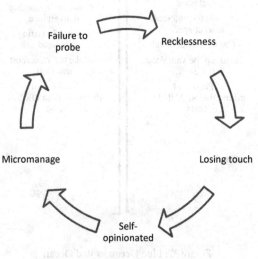

Figure 36: Formula for Failure

Blue Ocean Strategy

Blue Ocean Strategy, developed by Chan Kim and Renee Mauborgne, is a systematic approach to making competition irrelevant by creating uncontested market space. It aims to create and capture new demands while simultaneously pursue strategies of low differentiation and low costs. It provides a set of analytical tools and frameworks for companies to reshape their industry boundaries in their favour.

Kim and Mouborgne also coined the term *Red Ocean Strategy* to differentiate it from *Blue Ocean Strategy*. Their distinct differences are as presented in the diagram (Figure 37).

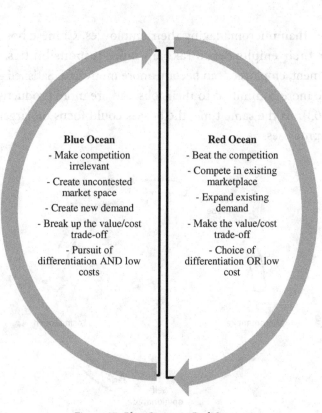

Figure 37: Blue Ocean vs Red Ocean

An important tool in *Blue Ocean Strategy* is the *Four Actions Framework* (Figure 38). The four actions are:

1) *Raising* those relevant factors above industry standards;
2) *Creating* factors that the industry has never offered;
3) *Reducing* factors that are below industry standards;
4) *Eliminating* factor that the industry has long competed on.

Through the *Four Actions Framework*, a new value curve as represented by an uncontested market space is created.

The concept of *Value Innovation* is the cornerstone of *Blue Ocean Strategy*. It is the simultaneous pursuit of differentiation and low costs.

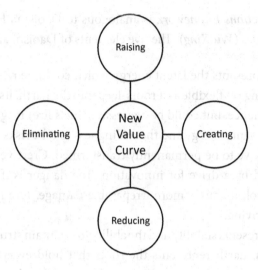

Figure 38: Four Actions Framework

It increases value to the company as well as the buyers by aligning the whole system of utility, price and costs. Cost savings are achieved by eliminating and reducing the factors an industry competes on. At the same time, buyer value is increased by creating new offerings to the buyers. This relationship is shown in Figure 39.

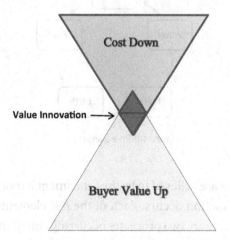

Figure 39: Value Innovation Strategies

The *Four Actions Framework* is analogous to Daoism's *Five Movements of Cosmic Energies* (*Wu Xing*). The five elements of Daoism are (Figure 40):

1) Wood — represents the latent energy which could be released and fuels fire. It is strong yet flexible as it roots deep into the Earth. Its characteristics is one of patience, but could be aggressive (fuels fire) if aggravated.
2) Fire — represents energy and the willingness to take risks. Old structures and habits have to be permanently transformed. Creative processes take place fuelled by a drive for innovation. The danger is if the fire grows out of control, it causes more irreparable damage. Fire needs Wood to continue thriving.
3) Earth — represents stability and the ability to maintain structural integrity under stress. Earth represents the roots that hold everything together. However, it can also become complacent and easily self-centred.
4) Metal — represents strength and hardness, but could change its form under pressure. It is often seen to be unyielding and resistant to change.
5) Water — represents the energy that flows throughout the organisation. It not only serves individual goal but the goal of the whole organisation as water flows into every gaps and openings.

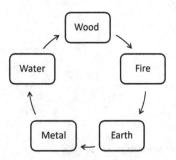

Figure 40: Five Elements

The five elements are believed to be the fundamental roots of the universe, between which interaction occurs. Each of the five elements influences and moulds the other. There are two processes occurring simultaneously: *Creation* and *Control*. The five elements maintain an inner equilibrium and harmony between the *Ying* and *Yang* energies throughout the creative cycle and control cycle. Figure 41 shows the relationships of the five elements in *Creation* and *Control* processes.

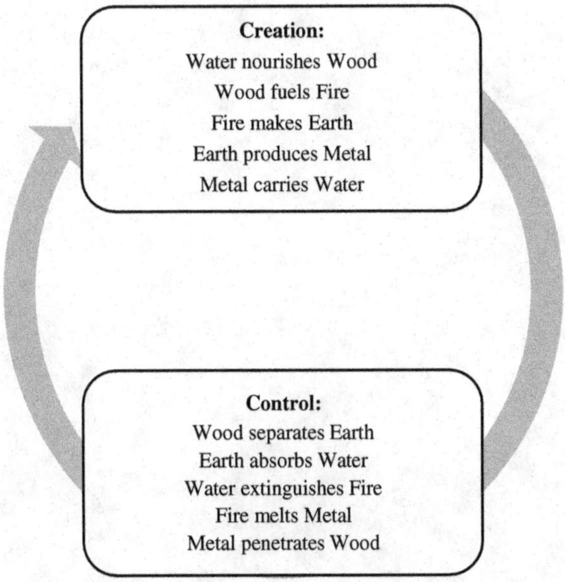

Creation:
Water nourishes Wood
Wood fuels Fire
Fire makes Earth
Earth produces Metal
Metal carries Water

Control:
Wood separates Earth
Earth absorbs Water
Water extinguishes Fire
Fire melts Metal
Metal penetrates Wood

Figure 41: Creation and Control

23

Army on the March

Sun Tzu said:

"We come now to the question of encamping the army, and observing signs of the enemy. Pass quickly over mountains, and keep in the neighborhood of valleys. Camp in high places, facing the sun. Do not climb heights in order to fight. So much for mountain warfare. After crossing a river, you should get far away from it.

When an invading force crosses a river in its onward march, do not advance to meet it in mid-stream. It will be best to let half the army get across, and then deliver your attack. If you are anxious to fight, you should not go to meet the invader near a river which he has to cross. Moor your craft higher up than the enemy, and facing the sun. Do not move up-stream to meet the enemy. So much for river warfare. In crossing salt-marshes, your sole concern should be to get over them quickly, without any delay.

If forced to fight in a salt-marsh, you should have water and grass near you, and get your back to a clump of trees. So much for operations in salt-

marches. In dry, level country, take up an easily accessible position with rising ground to your right and on your rear, so that the danger may be in front, and safety lie behind. So much for campaigning in flat country. These are the four useful branches of military knowledge which enabled the Yellow Emperor to vanquish four several sovereigns.

All armies prefer high ground to low and sunny places to dark. If you are careful of your men, and camp on hard ground, the army will be free from disease of every kind, and this will spell victory. When you come to a hill or a bank, occupy the sunny side, with the slope on your right rear.

Thus, you will at once act for the benefit of your soldiers and utilize the natural advantages of the ground. When, in consequence of heavy rains up-country, a river which you wish to ford is swollen and flecked with foam, you must wait until it subsides."

Business Applications

This chapter describes the different situations a manager faces and how he responds to these situations. He has to deal with various stakeholders and convince them of his ideas. To achieve this, he has to project an image of professionalism and confidence, even if he is in an adverse situation.

Good managers go through a passage where they experience trials and tribulations of failure. They become more resilient and develop the resolve to succeed. There are times when they face embarrassing or painful situations. What differentiates them from other people is that they learned from these experiences and come out as better managers.

As the Chinese proverb says, *"True gold fears no fire: a person of integrity can stand severe tests."*

Written in Chinese, "真金不怕红炉火。"

Leaders who do not succeed are those who lack self-awareness. They do not acknowledge their own lack of motivation and constantly find excuses

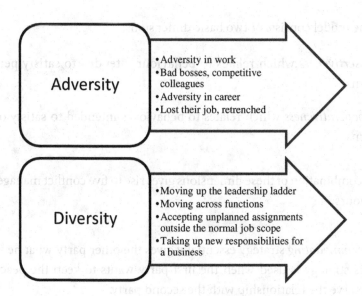

Figure 42: Passage of Leadership

for their failures. Good leaders and managers have to create conditions for growth. Their success or failure lies in their own hands. They have to go through periods of adversity, and at the same time expect diversity in their work and career (Figure 42).

Conflict Management Technique

Conflict management is an important skill to possess for all managers. Conflict normally arises from philosophical differences, divergent interests, power imbalances, or pure jealousy of another person.

Thomas and Kilmann (1974) developed the Conflict Mode Instrument that identified five common strategies to deal with conflict (Figure 43). Managers have to understand their own conflict management style and learn how to manage different situations using different approaches.

The model consists of two basic dimensions:

Assertiveness which relates to behaviour intended to satisfy personal concerns.

Cooperativeness which relates to behaviours intended to satisfy others' concerns.

A combination of these dimensions gives rise to five conflict management behaviours:

1) *Accommodating* strategy essentially gives the other party what he wants. This strategy is used when the first party wants to keep the peace and preserve the relationship with the second party.
2) *Avoiding* strategy is used to put off the conflict momentarily. The first party seeks to avoid a confrontation with the other party by withdrawing, sidestepping or delaying. This situation may also happen when it is not the right time to confront the issue. For example, a company may delay dismissing an unproductive employee before the new employee joins the company.
3) *Collaborating* strategy is used when the manager wishes to find a win-win solution to all parties. This form of conflict management style takes up a significant amount of time as it requires commitment from all parties.
4) *Compromising* strategy calls for both parties to give up certain elements of their positions to establish a mutually acceptable solution. This strategy prevails when both parties are equally strong in their negotiating positions.
5) *Competing* strategy is a power-oriented strategy in which one side wins and the other loses. One party may maintain his position aggressively. While such a strategy provides a quick resolution to a conflict situation, it may affect both parties' relationship in the long run as the dominant party tends to react in the same way in future situations.

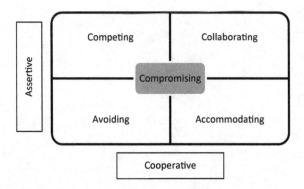

Figure 43: Conflict Mode Instrument

Sun Tzu said:

"Better prepare for confrontation than hope that the enemy will not come. Better ensure one's defense is impenetrable than hope that the enemy will not attack."

Likewise, managers who have good conflict management skills are able to manage conflicts before they escalate beyond repair.

Chapter

24

Classification of Terrain

Sun Tzu said:

"We may distinguish six kinds of terrain, to wit: (1) Accessible ground; (2) entangling ground; (3) temporizing ground; (4) narrow passes; (5) precipitous heights; (6) positions at a great distance from the enemy.

Ground which can be freely traversed by both sides is called accessible. With regard to ground of this nature, be before the enemy in occupying the raised and sunny spots, and carefully guard your line of supplies. Then you will be able to fight with advantage.

Ground which can be abandoned but is hard to re-occupy is called entangling. From a position of this sort, if the enemy is unprepared, you may sally forth and defeat him. But if the enemy is prepared for your coming, and you fail to defeat him, then, return being impossible, disaster will ensue.

When the position is such that neither side will gain by making the first move, it is called temporizing ground. In a position of this sort, even though the enemy should offer us an attractive bait, it will be advisable not to stir forth, but rather to retreat, thus enticing the enemy in his turn; then, when part of his army has come out, we may deliver our attack with advantage.

With regard to narrow passes, if you can occupy them first, let them be strongly garrisoned and await the advent of the enemy. Should the army forestall you in occupying a pass, do not go after him if the pass is fully garrisoned, but only if it is weakly garrisoned.

With regard to precipitous heights, if you are beforehand with your adversary, you should occupy the raised and sunny spots, and there wait for him to come up. If the enemy has occupied them before you, do not follow him, but retreat and try to entice him away.

If you are situated at a great distance from the enemy, and the strength of the two armies is equal, it is not easy to provoke a battle, and fighting will be to your disadvantage. These six are the principles connected with Earth. The general who has attained a responsible post must be careful to study them.

Now an army is exposed to six several calamities, not arising from natural causes, but from faults for which the general is responsible. These are: (1) Flight; (2) insubordination; (3) collapse; (4) ruin; (5) disorganization; (6) rout."

Business Applications

This chapter covers situational analysis of a company where the manager analyses both the internal and external environments affecting the company. With the right formula, managers are able to devise relevant plans to raise the competitive advantage and secure its vantage position in the market (Figure 44).

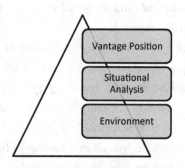

Figure 44: Situational Analysis

Internal environment refers to the company's products, people, market share, performance and positioning. It also includes business processes and culture of the company.

External environment could be further categorised as macro environment or micro environment. Macro relates to sociological, cultural, technological, economic and political factors. Micro environment refers to the structure of markets, consumer trends, and stakeholders.

Having a vantage point could literally mean possessing mental high ground. The traits of a successful manager include having strong moral values, personal integrity and motivation towards success.

Sun Tzu said:

"The Commander stands for the virtues of wisdom, sincerity, benevolence, courage, and strictness."

Likewise, a manager should be wise, sincere and fair to his subordinates if he wishes to earn their respect.

Incorporating McKinsey Matrix

The McKinsey Matrix is a strategy tool which helps multi-business organisations evaluate their portfolios and prioritise investments among different business units in a systematic manner. It is often used for brand marketing and product management.

There are two dimensions in the matrix: *Industry Attractiveness* and *Business Unit Strengths*.

Industry Attractiveness helps determine the attractiveness of the market by analysing the market size, the market growth rate, the number of competitors, market segmentation, labour and pricing trends.

Business Unit Strengths expresses the competitiveness of the company itself. This dimension comprises the company's market share, strength of its brand, profitability, customer loyalty, product differentiation and value chain.

There are three main strategies in the McKinsey Matrix — *grow, hold* and *harvest* (Figure 45).

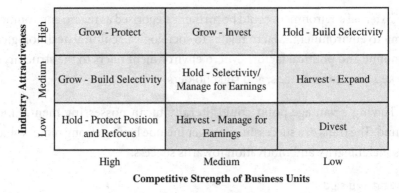

		High	Grow - Protect	Grow - Invest	Hold - Build Selectivity
Industry Attractiveness	Medium		Grow - Build Selectivity	Hold - Selectivity/ Manage for Earnings	Harvest - Expand
	Low		Hold - Protect Position and Refocus	Harvest - Manage for Earnings	Divest
			High	Medium	Low

Competitive Strength of Business Units

Figure 45: McKinsey Matrix

Grow strong business units in attractive industries, average business units in attractive industries and strong business units in average industries.

Hold average businesses in average industries, strong businesses in weak industries, and weak businesses in attractive industries.

Harvest weak business units in unattractive industries, average business units in unattractive industries, and weak business units in average industries.

Sun Tzu said:

"A superior leader who calculates the distance or proximity of dangers and obstructions and moves with confidence anywhere in his environment, is on the path to victory."

Likewise, a manager who carefully analyses the industry attractiveness will be able to achieve his performance above expectations.

Chapter

25

Nine Terrains

S un Tzu said:

"*The art of war recognizes nine varieties of ground: (1) Dispersive ground; (2) facile ground; (3) contentious ground; (4) open ground; (5) ground of intersecting highways; (6) serious ground; (7) difficult ground; (8) hemmed-in ground; (9) desperate ground.*

When a chieftain is fighting in his own territory, it is dispersive ground. When he has penetrated into hostile territory, but to no great distance, it is facile ground. Ground the possession of which imports great advantage to either side, is contentious ground. Ground on which each side has liberty of movement is open ground.

Ground which forms the key to three contiguous states, so that he who occupies it first has most of the Empire at his command, is a ground of intersecting highways.

When an army has penetrated into the heart of a hostile country, leaving a number of fortified cities in its rear, it is serious ground. Mountain forests, rugged steeps, marshes and fens — all country that is hard to traverse: this is difficult ground. Ground which is reached through narrow gorges, and from which we can only retire by tortuous paths, so that a small number of the enemy would suffice to crush a large body of our men: this is hemmed-in ground. Ground on which we can only be saved from destruction by fighting without delay, is desperate ground.

On dispersive ground, therefore, fight not. On facile ground, halt not. On contentious ground, attack not. On open ground, do not try to block the enemy's way. On the ground of intersecting highways, join hands with your allies. On serious ground, gather in plunder. In difficult ground, keep steadily on the march. On hemmed-in ground, resort to stratagem. On desperate ground, fight.

Those who were called skillful leaders of old knew how to drive a wedge between the enemy's front and rear; to prevent co-operation between his large and small divisions; to hinder the good troops from rescuing the bad, the officers from rallying their men. When the enemy's men were united, they managed to keep them in disorder. When it was to their advantage, they made a forward move; when otherwise, they stopped still.

If asked how to cope with a great host of the enemy in orderly array and on the point of marching to the attack, I should say: "Begin by seizing something which your opponent holds dear; then he will be amenable to your will. Rapidity is the essence of war: take advantage of the enemy's unreadiness, make your way by unexpected routes, and attack unguarded spots."

Business Applications

This chapter talks about the importance of *communication, cooperation* and *coordination* in achieving business success. The Triple C model which is often used in project management could be adapted as a tool for planning, organising and controlling of an organisation. To enhance the model, we could overlap it over the Triple Constraints model of *performance, time* and *costs* (Figure 46).

Enhanced Triple C Model

Figure 46: Enhanced Triple C Model

Communication channels, both internal and external, have to be kept open so that information flows are facilitated to all parties. Proper communication can also reduce the occurrence of miscommunication or misperception between parties. A breakdown in communication results in the misinterpretation of intended messages which could have financial and time implications. The common barriers to effective communication include:

1) Arrogance;
2) Lack of respect in the communicator;
3) Inattentiveness;
4) Technical jargons;
5) Lack of focus.

Cooperation is more than just consenting to work together. All parties involved have to be convinced of the merits of working together to achieve the common goal. Many failures occurred when the parties involved do not give their full commitment to the project. To facilitate cooperation, managers have to specify the following to all the relevant parties:

1) The achievable goals of the project;
2) The expected commitment from each individual;

3) Clear allocation of tasks to minimise conflict;
4) Documenting the merits of the project.

Coordination facilitates harmonious working relationships between the parties. With effective coordination, conflicts can be reduced to a minimal. It is often worthwhile to construct a responsibility chart to specify the reporting structure of the various parties. Managers have to indicate clearly the following:

1) What are the tasks of each individual?
2) What approval is needed?
3) Who is to give the approval?
4) Who is to report to whom of what?

The enhanced Triple C Model is highly useful in the context of Chinese management technique as its culture is one of High Power Distance Index. Subordinates may be reluctant to inform their superiors of negative news as they are afraid that they will be blamed for any faults. The model provides a framework to facilitate business processes and improve communication between all parties.

Sun Tzu said,

> "*If words of command are not clear and distinct, if orders are not thoroughly understood, then the general is to blame. But, if orders are clear and the soldiers nevertheless disobey, then it is the fault of their officers.*"

Sun Tzu noted that there are nine common stages in any campaign. The reaction to each stage of the campaign is highly applicable to business (Figure 47).

On *Home Ground* — this is the place where the business is most familiar with. However, managers should not be overly complacent and ignore the developments of the external environment.

On *Entering New Territory* — Managers have to plan well and analyse the new markets before investing too heavily into the market.

On *Contentious Ground* — Managers should survey the new markets first to determine the strength of the competitors. They should not let the competitors know of their true intentions to enter a new market.

On *Open Ground* — Managers should not confront competitors directly to avoid unnecessary wastage of resources.

On *Intersecting Ground* — Managers should collaborate and form strategic alliances where possible in areas where there are interested parties of equal strengths.

On *Serious Ground* — This is a scenario where the manager finds it hard to either move forward or background. The best strategy for him is to maintain his ground by developing relationships with various stakeholders.

On *Difficult Ground* — Managers have to maximize the employees' productivity to keep the company competitive. They have to constantly upgrade and innovate, pushing for new targets.

On *Hemmed-in Ground* — This is a situation where the manager feels entrapped or confined to his current position. To extricate himself, he has to resort to deception, intrigue and stratagem.

On *Desperate Ground* — In such a situation, the manager finds that there is no other alternative for him. He has to give it his all. It is about survival.

Sun Tzu said:

"Seize opportunities so that others do not gain. Take paths that are unexpected. Attack locations that are unprotected. Speed presides over the conditions of strategy, when a swift challenge is necessary for survival. And delay results in extinction."

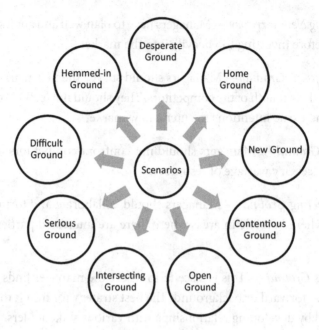

Figure 47: Nine Situations

Case of Groupon

Choosing the wrong partner or not picking the right partner can be a very costly experience for foreign companies. Groupon's (a U.S. online coupon company) partnership with Tencent was ill-fated as the former failed to take advantage of Tencent's resources. It entered China in 2011 via a joint venture company, Gaopeng. Both Groupon and Tencent have equal shares of 40% each in the joint venture with the remaining owned by Rocket Asia (10%) and Yunfeng (10%). Groupon adopted a strategy of enticing competitors' employees with high salaries to join the company.

Gaopeng recently announced that it has secured another round of financing from Groupon and Tencent. The investment is believed to be over USD30 million. This makes Gaopeng to be the only group-buying company to secure new investments recently in light of the closures of many smaller competitors.

Group-buying or *tuangou* (团购) has been popularised in China since 2005. *Tuangou* enables groups of consumers to purchase vouchers online that offer huge discounts, ranging from restaurants to airline tickets. These vouchers are available for a limited period of time and often create impulse buying. Consumers are drawn to *tuangou* not only by discounts but also by the range of products available such as jewelry and automobiles.

There are three types of *tuangou* in China. The first are independent websites backed by venture investors. This category includes Meituan, Lashou, Groupon.cn (a clone of Groupon.com) and Gaopeng. The second are channels that span leading social networking sites such as Taobao, Renren and Dianping. The third are aggregators or consolidators of group-buying sites.

Intense competition from more than 4,000 local group buying sites forced Gaopeng to shrink its operation. It insisted on an equal 50/50 revenue sharing with merchants in China without understanding that Chinese group buying websites sacrifice profits for more clients. It had to lay off more than 400 employees. Groupon continued to manage its China's operation by hiring Westerners and managing Chinese employees the American way. The failure of Groupon to adapt to the local market and the lack of communication with local employees forced Groupon to shut down unprofitable branches in China.

In China, retrenchments are not too common. Unlike the United States, mutual trust between employees and employer is more important than employment contracts (Fan & Zhang, 2004). International managers have to understand the cultural sensitivities of Chinese workers when making decisions in their organisations. China is becoming a very attractive market for foreign businesses due to the large population and also as a sourcing location. Forming strategic alliances is a popular mode of entry into the market for most foreign enterprises (Albaum, *et al.*, 2010).

Fiery Attack

S un Tzu said:

"There are five ways of attacking with fire. The first is to burn soldiers in
their camp; the second is to burn stores; the third is to burn baggage trains;
the fourth is to burn arsenals and magazines; the fifth is to hurl dropping
fire amongst the enemy.

In order to carry out an attack, we must have means available. The material
for raising fire should always be kept in readiness. There is a proper season
for making attacks with fire, and special days for starting a conflagration. The
proper season is when the weather is very dry; the special days are those when
the moon is in the constellations of the Sieve, the Wall, the Wing or the Cross-
bar; for these four are all days of rising wind.

In attacking with fire, one should be prepared to meet five possible
developments: (1) When fire breaks out inside to enemy's camp, respond at
once with an attack from without. (2) If there is an outbreak of fire, but the

enemy's soldiers remain quiet, bide your time and do not attack. (3) When the force of the flames has reached its height, follow it up with an attack, if that is practicable; if not, stay where you are. (4) If it is possible to make an assault with fire from without, do not wait for it to break out within, but deliver your attack at a favorable moment. (5) When you start a fire, be to windward of it. Do not attack from the leeward. A wind that rises in the daytime lasts long, but a night breeze soon falls.

In every army, the five developments connected with fire must be known, the movements of the stars calculated, and a watch kept for the proper days. Hence those who use fire as an aid to the attack show intelligence; those who use water as an aid to the attack gain an accession of strength. By means of water, an enemy may be intercepted, but not robbed of all his belongings. Unhappy is the fate of one who tries to win his battles and succeed in his attacks without cultivating the spirit of enterprise; for the result is waste of time and general stagnation. Hence the saying: The enlightened ruler lays his plans well ahead; the good general cultivates his resources."

Business Applications

This chapter talks about fierce competitive engagement. Sun Tzu advised the following:

1) Compete only to win. The best strategy is to win without competing. To achieve this, managers have to master the art of psychological warfare by discouraging the other party to compete directly. Two possible scenarios may happen. The competitor may reassess its entry into the market or it may wish to form a strategic alliance with the company. Winning without competing requires a combination of carefully thought out strategies (Figure 48). These include:

   a. Strong leadership;
   b. Good business intelligence;
   c. Knowledge of the market and competitor;
   d. Swift penetration into the market;
   e. Forming strategic alliances.

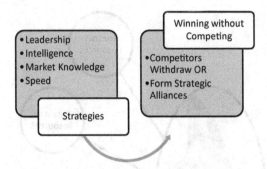

Figure 48: Winning without Competing

2) Do not compete if there is little chance of winning. Managers have to understand the various stakeholders of their competitors: suppliers, logistics operators, customers, financiers, etc. Try to build relationships with these stakeholders and disrupt the competitors' alliances with the stakeholders. This could be achieved by offering them better terms and conditions if they establish a new relationship with the company. Disrupting the supply chain of the competitors could reduce their production schedule, market share, profitability, and credibility. Figure 49 illustrates the different modes of attack.

3) Challenge to win and attack to control market share. Managers have to gather competitive intelligence about their competitors. Analyse their recent moves to predict their strategies. They have to establish if there are certain patterns pre-empting the next move of their competitors.

Sun Tzu's strategies are similar to strategies proposed by Western management guru, Philip Kotler. The latter suggested six ways to mount strategic offences:

1) Attack competitors' strengths;
2) Attack competitors' weaknesses;
3) Simultaneous attacks on multiple fronts;
4) End-run offensives (head-on);
5) Guerrilla offensives;
6) Pre-emptive strikes.

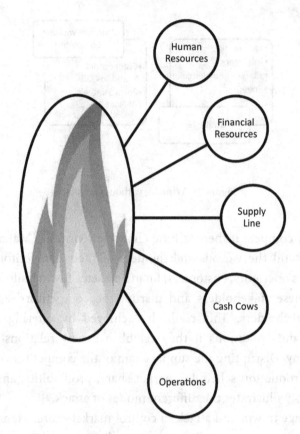

Figure 49: Fiery Attack

End-run offensives involve manoeuvring around competitors and capturing unoccupied or less congested territories. A company could launch new products in those areas where its competitors have little presence. Another strategy is to introduce next-generation technologies to leapfrog competitors.

Guerrilla offensives take the form of intense sporadic promotional activities to surprise the competitors. Such activities are normally targeted at cost conscious customers looking for good bargains.

Pre-emptive strikes involve securing positions that rivals may find difficult to duplicate. The first mover advantage gives the company access to the best suppliers, distributors and customers in the market.

Value Chain Analysis

Achieving competitive advantage over competitors entails outmanaging them along the value chain and finding creative ways to reduce overall costs. The Value Chain Analysis is a model developed by Michael Porter to describe the processes by which a company identifies each stage of its production process and which steps can be eliminated or improvements be made. By carefully analysing the internal activities, the manager should be able to reveal where the firm's competitive advantages or disadvantages are. It can achieve advantage by differentiating its products or services, performing internal activities at lower costs, offering more superior products and services, and reducing its costs of production.

The processes in Value Chain Analysis are also reflected in Sun Tzu's teachings. He listed the strategies for companies to deal with fierce competition which we discussed earlier in this chapter. Companies have to identify their strengths and chances of winning in a competition.

Sun Tzu said:

"When you know yourself but not the enemy, your chances of winning and losing are equal."

He had advised the need to have an effective information system. The flow of information could be either formal or informal, and it is essential to validate the sources of the information.

Timing plays a critical role in achieving success. The smooth flow of raw materials to the factories or finished goods to end customers can have a significant impact on the sales and profitability of the company. Any disruption to the supply chain can have an adverse impact on the operations and financial well-being of the firm.

Sun Tzu said:

"When the strike of the hawk breaks the body of its prey, it is because of timing. The timing is similar to the release of the trigger."

There are two main components in Value Chain Analysis (Figure 50). They are:

1) Primary Activities

    a. Inbound Logistics
    b. Operations
    c. Outbound Logistics
    d. Marketing & Sales
    e. Services

2) Supporting Activities

    a. Firm Infrastructure
    b. Human Resource Management
    c. Technology
    d. Procurement

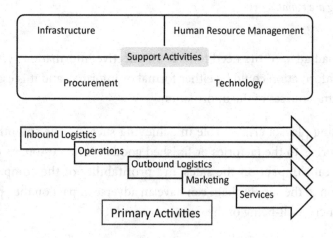

Figure 50: Value Chain Analysis

Case of Dalian Wanda Group

Dalian Wanda Group is investing RMB35 billion (SGD7 billion) in Hefei, Anhui Province, to compete with Disney's USD5.5 billion (SGD7.5 billion) resort in Shanghai. Wanda's development will include a theme park, hotels, a movie theatre, a shopping mall and residential apartments. The company plans to open 59 new theme parks across China by 2020. Unlike Disney, Wanda has localised its theme parks featuring local architectural styles. With an entrance fee of RMB200 compared to Disney's RMB499, Wanda hopes to capture a large segment of budget conscious visitors.

Wanda Group is determined to overtake Disney as the world's largest tourism group in four years' time. It has bought Hollywood's Legendary Entertainment for USD3.5 billion and is in discussion to buy Carmike Cinemas in the United States. In addition, it has recently established a partnership with Sony Pictures to invest in movie productions.

Disney is aware of the difficulties of operating in China as evidenced from the closure of its video streaming service just after five months in operation. However, China with its large population base still proves to be an attractive market for the company.

Other Chinese companies which have invested in Hollywood production houses include Fosun International which acquired a stake in Studio 8 and Huayi Brothers Media Corp's partnership with STX Entertainment.

While Wanda has a strong foothold in China, it nevertheless faces mounting pressures from competitors both from China and from overseas. It may be helpful for the company to embrace ambiguity in the business environment with paradoxical management views (Figure 51).

The Greek philosopher Aristotle advocated the concept of *golden mean*, which is the desired path between two extremes. For example, courage taken to one extreme leads to recklessness, while to the other extreme leads to cowardice. A similar concept was noted in the *Analects of Confucius*:

> *"The Master [Confucius] said, 'The virtue embodied in the doctrine of the Mean is of the highest order. But it has long been rare among people.'"*

Likewise, Buddha expressed the Middle Way as to describe the Noble Eightfold Path as the way to achieving nirvana, instead of employing extremes of self-indulgence. Buddha said:

> *"A middle path, avoiding two extremes have been discovered by Tathagata — a path which opens the eyes, and bestows understanding, which leads to peace of mind, to the higher wisdom, to full enlightenment, to Nirvana."*

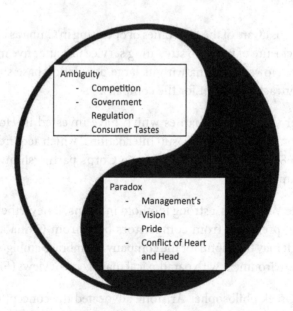

Figure 51: Balancing Ambiguity and Paradoxical Views

Chapter
27

Employing Spies

Sun Tzu said:

"Raising a host of a hundred thousand men and marching them great distances entails heavy loss on the people and a drain on the resources of the State. The daily expenditure will amount to a thousand ounces of silver. There will be commotion at home and abroad, and men will drop down exhausted on the highways. As many as seven hundred thousand families will be impeded in their labor.

Hostile armies may face each other for years, striving for the victory which is decided in a single day. This being so, to remain in ignorance of the enemy's condition simply because one grudges the outlay of a hundred ounces of silver in honors and emoluments, is the height of inhumanity. One who acts thus is no leader of men, no present help to his sovereign, no master of victory. Thus, what enables the wise sovereign and the good general to strike and conquer, and achieve things beyond the reach of ordinary men, is foreknowledge.

Now this foreknowledge cannot be elicited from spirits; it cannot be obtained inductively from experience, nor by any deductive calculation. Knowledge of the enemy's dispositions can only be obtained from other men. Hence the use of spies, of whom there are five classes: (1) Local spies; (2) inward spies; (3) converted spies; (4) doomed spies; (5) surviving spies.

When these five kinds of spy are all at work, none can discover the secret system. This is called "divine manipulation of the threads". It is the sovereign's most precious faculty. Having local spies means employing the services of the inhabitants of a district. Having inward spies, making use of officials of the enemy. Having converted spies, getting hold of the enemy's spies and using them for our own purposes. Having doomed spies, doing certain things openly for purposes of deception, and allowing our spies to know of them and report them to the enemy. Surviving spies, finally, are those who bring back news from the enemy's camp.

Hence it is that which none in the whole army are more intimate relations to be maintained than with spies. None should be more liberally rewarded. In no other business should greater secrecy be preserved. Spies cannot be usefully employed without a certain intuitive sagacity. They cannot be properly managed without benevolence and straightforwardness. Without subtle ingenuity of mind, one cannot make certain of the truth of their reports. Be subtle! Be subtle! And use your spies for every kind of business."

Business Applications

This chapter focuses on the importance of gathering good information sources and managing business intelligence. Managers need to have up-to-date information on customers' preferences, competitors' strengths and market trends. Sun Tzu noted that five kinds of spies are used in war. They are:

1) Local Spies — those close to the target company;
2) Inward Spies — normally disgruntled employees of the target company who resent their management;
3) Converted Spies — spies of the target company (double-agent);

4) Doomed Spies — compromised company's spies who are given false information;
5) Surviving Spies — company's spies who work for the target company and are able to escape detection.

Good and reliable information is critical to business success. It is essential for the manager to develop a network that can provide the required information. All information has to be filtered to distinguish the relevant and irrelevant information.

However, companies should be aware that information obtained through illegal means such as industrial espionage or computer hacking can do significant damage to the credibility of the company.

Legally obtained sources of information may be internal or external to the target company (Figure 52).

Internal sources include:

1) Company reports;
2) Stock analysis;
3) Existing employees;
4) Competitors contacts (suppliers, customers, business partners).

External sources include:

1) Market research documents;
2) Magazine and journal publications;
3) Government statistics;
4) Trade publications.

Sun Tzu said:

"With advance information, costly mistake can be avoided, destruction averted, and the way to lasting victory made clear. Subtly, very subtly, do not neglect the use of intelligence."

Figure 52: Sources of Business Intelligence

Section 5

Japanese Management Styles

Chapter

28

Japanese Philosophy

J apanese philosophy is largely a fusion of Confucianism, Buddhism and Western philosophies. Confucianism and Buddhism were introduced into Japan around the fifth century A.D. The influence of Confucianism is prevalent in the areas of social structure, government and ethics. The concept of loyalty and honour advocated by Confucius had a strong impact within the Japanese *samurai* or warrior class in the 16th century. The dyadic relationships between master-servant, parent-child, husband-wife, elder sibling-younger sibling and friend-friend, had been widely practiced by the imperial family.

Buddhism entered Japan from Korea. There are three schools of Japanese Buddhism. They are:

1) Zen Buddhism — belief that all beings have a nature of inherent wisdom and virtue, which lies deep in the mind;
2) Pure Land Buddhism — belief that through Amitabha Buddha, one would be reborn in Pure Land where enlightenment is assured;
3) Nichiren Buddhism — belief that enlightenment is attainable in the current form and present lifetime. This is the message in the Lotus Sutra.

The philosophical influence of Buddhism is obvious in these areas: psychology, metaphysics and aesthetics. In psychology, Buddhism helps to bring awareness of the workings of the heart and mind. In metaphysics, it helps raise the question about ultimate nature of reality. The understanding of the natural world and the metaphysical principles of expression became the underlying principles for Japanese aesthetics.

Many Japanese follow both Shintoism and Buddhism. Shintoism is a type of polytheistic animism. According to Shintoism, humanity and nature are part of each other, and not independent existing entities. Within Shintoism, the Buddha is another Kami (nature deity) while Buddhism regards Kami as manifestations of various Buddhas and Bodhisattvas.

The four affirmations in Shintoism are:

1) Tradition and family;
2) Love of nature;
3) Physical cleanliness;
4) Matsuri (Honour gods and ancestral spirits).

The concept of spiritual immanence instead of transcendence has remained strong in Japanese thoughts up to today.

Western philosophies became popular in Japan in the middle of the 19th century as the government realised there is an urgent need to modernise Japan and to relate Western concepts to Japanese thoughts. Japan managed to organise an industrial capitalist state based on Western model. Contemporary Japanese philosopher Nishida Kitaro argued for the synthesis of Western and Eastern philosophies through epistemological analysis.

Chapter

29

Japanese Management Practices

Japanese organisations are quite similar to Western organisations in that they have a *kaichoa* (chairman) at the helm, a *shachoh* (president), *fuku shahchoh* (vice president), *senmu torishimariyaku* (managing director) and *torishimariyaku* (directors).

Below them are the *buchoh* (departmental managers), *buchoh dairi* (deputy managers), *kachohi* (section managers) and *kari kachoi* (supervisors). Figure 53 illustrates a typical Japanese organisational structure.

Japanese management encourages information to flow from the ground to top management. This kind of management style is more supervisory than hands-on. As such, it has often been criticised that senior executives do not fully understand the problems faced by workers.

Decision-making in many Japanese organisations is based on the culture of collectivism and shared responsibilities. This is the fundamental concept of the *ringi* system which is based on *nemawashi* or consensual decision-making. *Ringi* or formal authorisation procedure involves four stages: proposal,

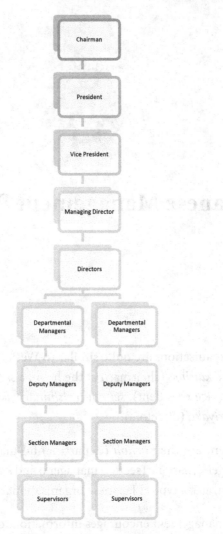

Figure 53: Typical Organisational Structure

circulation, approval and record. A *ringisho* or proposal document is circulated to all employees involved at the lower levels before submitting upwards to senior management (Figure 54).

Strategies are organised by those directly connected with the changes. They are then brought up for discussions with successive levels of management before the top management makes the final decision. This is a long and time-consuming process (Sethi & Namiki, 1984). When a project fails, the top

Figure 54: The *Ringi* Process

management has to bear the brunt of the blame although rewards from the project are shared with the lower-level employees.

Under Japanese Commercial Law, the *torishimariyakukai* (board of directors) occupies the apex position in the organisation. They are responsible for choosing a *daihyo torishimariyaku* (representative director) to act on their behalf for daily activities. In Japan, there are few external directors. Senior executives such as chief of factories or head of technical departments may also be nominated as directors.

Japanese employees also tend to remain in their companies longer than their Western counterparts as they see loyalty to their companies as one form of job security. This is important as companies need a stable workforce for their operations. The offer of *shushinkoyo* or lifetime employment also means that employees are less motivated to look for new employment elsewhere. Hiring of new employees may involve a long and detailed process of screening ranging from assessing academic qualifications, conducting checks on family backgrounds, and personal interviews. Most Japanese firms consider the potential ability of the new candidate rather than whether he is suitable for specific jobs.

However, in modern-day Japan, permanent employment is becoming increasingly less as temporary workers or those working for smaller organisations do not get to enjoy job security. Even lower-level or technical employees in large companies are not assured of permanent employment. Continuous training is a norm in Japan as workers obtain new skills as part of his job until he retires. This continuous training prevents extreme specialisation and departmentalisation of Japanese workers. As such, Japanese workers are generalists and are more adaptable to new tasks than their Western counterparts.

In many Japanese companies, a selection for promotion is conducted within each *nenji* (cohort). While tenure-based management of promotion see all selected managers being promoted, their degree of promotion may differ over time. Staff with specialised skills are assigned managerial positions while those with no managerial positions are given the title of "specialist".

Because of the early retirement age at 55, many government bureaucrats join large business organisations after retirement, a pattern refer to as *amakudari*. Large organisations normally recruit retired government officials who have good connection to the major ministries that they have dealings with. While *amakudari* officials play an important role of communicating directly with their former ministries, they also facilitate corruption as many important decision-making procedures are bypassed. High profile *amakudari*-related scandals include Japan Highway Public Corporation, Narita Airport, and Tokyo Electric Power Company.

Japan experienced a phenomenal industrial growth after the World War II. The government focused on certain industries to grow rather than covering a broad spectrum of industries. In the initial years, Japan imported their technology instead of investing in Research and Development. They negotiated licensing agreements and directed their efforts to production. This emphasis on productivity has earned them a reputation of producing quality products. For many years, Japan had imitated Western products as it copied as well as learned at the same time good product designs and quality image.

Case of Fanuc

Fanuc is a leading manufacturing of factory automation systems, equipment and robots. Its main competitors are Japan's Yaskawa Electric, Switzerland's ABB and Germany's Kuka. The company is headed by Yoshiharu Inaba, who served as the Chairman and CEO.

Yoshiharu Inaba spends most of his time talking to his clients and rarely engages with shareholders citing that the time talking to outsiders could be used to meet another customer. In line with Prime Minister's Shinzo Abe's call for broader corporate governance, Fanuc will increase its numbers of outside directors on the board. At the same time, it will open up to investors and seek to improve shareholders return. Abenomics calls for companies to deploy more cash to reinvigorate Japan's economy. For many shareholders, there is a veil of secrecy about the company and the new legislation is a move in the right direction to get Japanese corporations to be more transparent.

Lao Tzu said:

"Time is a created thing. To say 'I don't have time', is like saying, 'I don't want to'."

David Herro of Oakmark International Fund and former Fanuc shareholder, said:

"They are less prone to grant access to management than most companies in Japan or the world. It's a very good business, but they run that thing like it's a family farm."

Fanuc's more open approach to investors could be partly due to the pressures from Daniel Loeb which operates hedge fund Third Point. Daniel Loeb criticised Fanuc for hoarding too much cash and urged the company to make better use of its USD6.8 billion cash hoard. In response, Fanuc announced that it would double its dividends and buy back stocks.

Perhaps, the best strategy for the company to deal with investors and to portray the image of playing a role of boosting Japan's economy through active investments is "thinking big while acting small". To think big such as making global expansion plans requires inputs of smaller sub-plans. To achieve overall vision requires smaller steps or building blocks which fit together (Figure 55).

Lao Tzu said:

"A journey of a thousand miles begins with a single step."

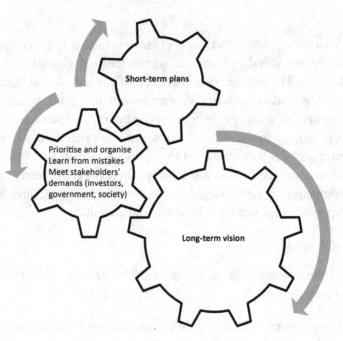

Short-term plans

Prioritise and organise
Learn from mistakes
Meet stakeholders'
demands (investors,
government, society)

Long-term vision

Figure 55: Think Big, Act Small

Chapter 30

Just-In-Time Manufacturing

Japan adopted the manufacturing technique of Just-In-Time (JIT) and Total Quality Management. JIT manufacturing was popularised by Toyota to reduce flow times within production as well as response times from suppliers and to customers. The father of JIT is Taiichi Ohno.

The success of JIT in Japan could be explained by the strong work ethics of Japanese employees. Japanese companies encourage their workers to continually strive for improvements and achieving higher standards. Quality circles is another concept popularised in Japan where teams come together to share ideas and solve problems. These quality circles consist of around 10 workers who meet regularly to discuss work-related matters.

The main advantage of JIT is that it frees up resources which could be employed elsewhere. For example, warehouse space which would otherwise be used for inventory storage could be freed up for office or retail space. Reorder levels for certain items are set, and new stocks are ordered when the levels are reached. On the other hand, JIT also poses challenges to companies. Companies have to rethink the entire workflow and locate to near its suppliers or customers. Companies which produce small quantities may not enjoy the full benefits of JIT as suppliers may be reluctant to supply small quantities of materials at low costs. As JIT is based on current or past sales figures, companies may also not be able to meet customers' orders if there is a sudden surge in demands.

The fundamental principles of JIT are the pull system (what is needed), the continuous flow processing, and the *takt* time. Under the pull system, the quantity of work performed at each stage of the production is dictated by the demand for materials from the immediate next stage (Figure 56).

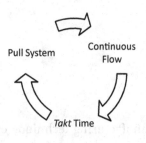

Figure 56: JIT

Advantages and Disadvantages of JIT

While Toyota plays a major role in popularising JIT in the 1970s, the concept originated at Ford Motors Company in the 1920s. Many Western companies such as General Motors, Dell and Harley Davidson have also leveraged on JIT principles as part of their manufacturing processes. Over the years, the concept has been modified by other companies and we have seen variations of *lean* management and quality management tools. Hewlett Packard called it "stockless production" while Motorola developed the "Six Sigma" tools.

The advantages and disadvantages of JIT are listed in Table 3. Figure 57 also illustrates the advantages of JIT.

Table 3: Advantages and Disadvantages of JIT

Advantages	Disadvantages
Minimise waste (materials, equipment, parts, space, workers' time)	Negative impact to production if supplier's delivery is delayed
Satisfy customers' needs with timely delivery	Need to integrate closely the company's and supplier's computer systems so that they can coordinate the delivery of parts and materials
Improved cash flows as money is not tied up in stocks	Machine and manpower may be left idle when there is no production
Discuss work practices, consultations and cooperation rather than confrontation	Companies may not be able to meet a surge in order from customers since they have little stocks or finished goods
Expose problems rather than covering them up	May be difficult and expensive to implement JIT system
Develop close relationships with suppliers	Little room for mistake as minimal stock is kept for production
Improve stock management and minimise inventory obsolescence	Companies may not have the market intelligence to predict market demands as some industries are more volatile than others
Easier to halt production and switch to different products if customers' needs change	Companies are more susceptible to changing raw materials prices as they do not stockpile the materials

The Japanese also use a self-regulation production control system known as *Kanban*. The *Kanban* system is sometimes called the "supermarket method" because it borrowed the concept from supermarkets. The latter use product control cards containing information such as product names, codes and storage location. The maximum amount of time in which a product needs to be produced in order to satisfy customer demand is known as the *takt* time. The term is derived from the German word *Taktzeit*, which is often referred to as the heartbeat of production in *lean* manufacturing.

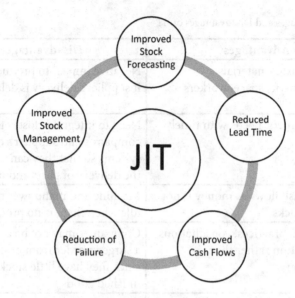

Figure 57: Advantages of JIT

There are two types of *Kanban*:

a) Production *Kanban* which signals the need to produce more parts. Each Kanban is attached to a container.

b) Retrieval *Kanban* which signals the need to retrieve parts from one work centre and deliver them to the next work centre.

Figure 58 shows the relationship between production *Kanban* and retrieval *Kanban*.

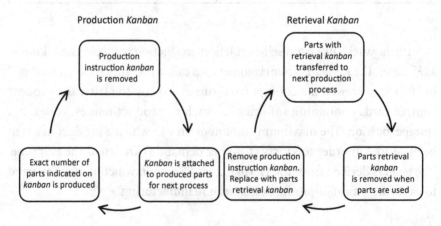

Figure 58: *Kanban* Systems

Through a number of quality control techniques, quality is maximised and wastes minimised. These techniques are *jidoka*, and *poka-yoke*. *Jidoka* refers to automation with a human touch. In *jidoka*, when an error occurs, everything stops. This implies quality is controlled at the source (Figure 59).

The practice of *poka-yoke* ensures that mistakes are prevented by designing manufacturing process, equipment and tools so that an operation cannot be performed incorrectly. Devices such as jigs, gadgets and warning systems are attached to machines to automatically check for abnormalities in the manufacturing process.

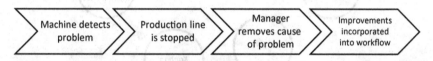

Figure 59: Concept of *Jidoka*

Both *jidoka* and *poka-yoke* have been repackaged into *Lean* management techniques. *Lean* manufacturing is a management philosophy which takes into account the elimination of waste within a manufacturing system (Figure 60).

The concept was promoted by Toyota to improve the flow of work. Heijunka (production levelling) is a technique to eliminate *mura* (unevenness) which in turn reduces *muda* (waste) throughout the manufacturing system. The role of lean leaders is to coach and mentor less experienced lean champions. This is emphasised in the concepts of *senpai* (senior), *kohai* (junior) and *sensei* (teacher).

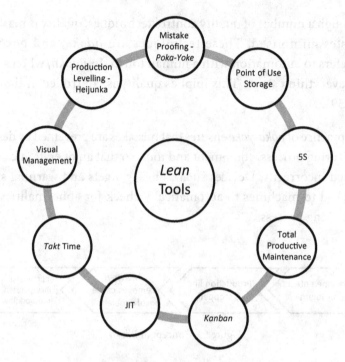

Figure 60: Lean Manufacturing

Chapter 31

Kaizen

Continuous improvements centre around two principles:

1) *Kaizen* is a philosophy that sees improvement in productivity as a gradual and methodical process. Operations must be improved continuously with innovation and evolution. *Kaizen* 5-S framework is an approach to solving business problems. The 5S are:

   a. Sustain — Maintaining established processes;
   b. Set-in-order — Orderliness, easy retrieval of items;
   c. Shine — Cleanliness in the workplace;
   d. Standardise — Utilising standard approach for task completion;
   e. Sort — Separate those needed items from unneeded items.

The benefits of adopting the 5S framework are less waste, reduction of space, improvements in maintenance, improvement in quality, and increased employee commitment. Figure 61 illustrates the *Kaizen* 5S framework.

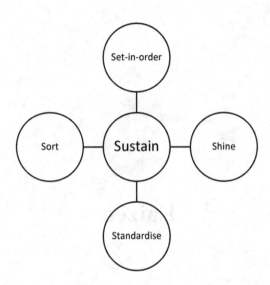

Figure 61: *Kaizen* 5S Framework

2) *Genchi genbutsu* involves going to the source and seeing for oneself. It is quite similar to the Western concept of *Management by Walking about* (MBWA). Both *genchi genbutsu* and MBWA stress that the only way to understand the problem is to go to the ground and see it for oneself. When a problem arises, go to the *gemba* (place) first, check the *genbutsu* (relevant objects), and find the cause of the problem. Figure 62 illustrates the process of *genchi genbutsu* of a continuously learning organisation.

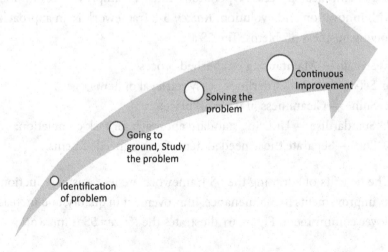

Figure 62: *Genchi Genbutsu*

Toyota Production System

The Toyota Production System includes various concepts discussed above: JIT, *jidoka*, *heijunka*, *kanban*, *kaizen* and *nemawashi*. JIT and *Jidoka* are the two pillars of Toyota's Production System (Figure 63).

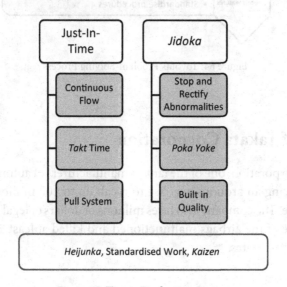

Figure 63: Toyota Production System

Just-In-Time (JIT) manufacturing focuses on production efficiency while *lean* manufacturing goes a step further and examines it from the perspective of customers' value. In *lean* manufacturing, we consider which aspects of the products add real value for the customers. For example, the customer buying a car is looking for design, performance and safety. The principle of *lean* manufacturing is that every step in the production process must add value to the customer.

Toyota has introduced a number of procedures to resolve production problems. The problem-solving process is shown in Figure 64.

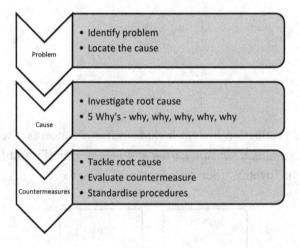

Figure 64: Toyota's Problem-Solving Process

Case of Takata Corporation

Takata Corporation, one of the largest manufacturers of automobile air bags is facing an arduous exercise to recall up to 100 million airbags worldwide. The company also faces millions of dollars of legal liabilities after some of the airbags malfunctioned and killed at least 15 people in the United States.

Takata's customers include Honda Motor Co., Toyota Motor Corp., Nissan Motor Co., General Motors Co., BMW AG, Dimamler AG, Ford Motor Co., Fiat Chrysler Automobile NV, Jaguar Rover Automotive PLC and Volkswagen AG.

The negative news has impacted Takata's share price over the past year, reducing the market capitalisation by almost 70% to USD285 million as of September 2016. The company is in a quandary as automakers are reluctant to help foot part of Takata's legal bill. Without an injection of new funds, the company risks facing bankruptcy proceedings as the costs of recalling all non-desiccated airbag inflators are estimated to be more than JPY1.28 trillion.

The U.S. National Transport Safety Administration had published reports that Takata failed to report problems with the airbags when they first arose. One of the measures that the company has taken is creating several new positions — a Chief Safety and Accountability Officer and a Vice President for Ethics and Compliance.

This is quite appalling in view of the fact that most Japanese manufacturers stress on *Kaizen* as one of their manufacturing philosophies.

33

Theory Z

Williams Ouchi detailed Theory Z in his 1981 book, *Theory Z: How American Management Can Meet the Japanese Challenge*. The theory combines the best of Japanese and Western philosophies. He emphasised that the secret to success lies in the way employees are managed. If employees are engaged and empowered, they become more productive. He argued that organisations should adopt the following:

1) Strong company philosophy and culture to convince employees that they have ownership of their work;
2) Staff development and training;
3) Consensus in decision-making to encourage staff to take part in organisational decisions;
4) "Generalist" employees with specialised career responsibilities;
5) Concern for well-being of employees;
6) Informal control with formal measures to assess work quality and performance;
7) Individual responsibilities and team responsibilities.

Differences with Theories X and Y

Theory X and Theory Y were proposed by Douglas McGregor in his 1960 book, *The Human Side of Enterprise*. Theory X is an authoritarian management style which states that employees dislike work and have to be enticed to work. They also need supervision at all levels. Theory X organizations are heavily bureaucratic with little delegation of responsibilities.

Conversely, Theory Y states that employees view work as part of life. They work best when they are left alone. They will use their own creativity to solve problems and seek out responsibilities and new tasks. Theory Y is a participative management style which assumes that workers could be motivated to achieve higher levels.

Figure 65 shows the comparisons of the three theories X, Y and Z.

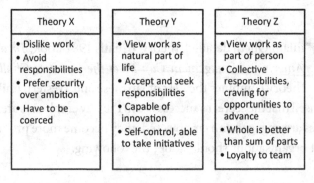

Theory X	Theory Y	Theory Z
• Dislike work • Avoid responsibilities • Prefer security over ambition • Have to be coerced	• View work as natural part of life • Accept and seek responsibilities • Capable of innovation • Self-control, able to take initiatives	• View work as part of person • Collective responsibilities, craving for opportunities to advance • Whole is better than sum of parts • Loyalty to team

Figure 65: Theories X, Y, and Z

Critics of Japanese management system see a system that often restricts employees' freedom of expression. As a result, Japanese employees are highly stressed. They argue that stress is also caused when managers delegate and pass responsibilities to employees. The push for continuous improvements through *kaizen* and *lean* production causes stress level to increase significantly (Conti *et al.*, 2006).

Kiretsu System

The collapse of *zaibatsu* (family-controlled vertical monopolies) following World War II gave rise to *kiretsu*. A *kiretsu* essentially is a system or groupings of enterprises with interlocking business relationships and shareholders. There are two forms of *kiretsu*: classical *kiretsu* and vertically integrated *kiretsu*.

There are six big classical *kiretsu* (also known as horizontal or financial *kiretsu*) in Japan. They are the Fuyo Group, Sumitomo, Sanwa, Mitsui, Mistubishi and Daiichi-Kangyo Ginko. Classical *kiretsu* are centred around a bank through cross-sharing relationships with other companies (Figure 66). There is no focus on any specific industry.

Vertical *kiretsu* (also known as industrial *kiretsu*) focuses on a single industry and links suppliers, manufacturers and distributors. Examples of vertical *kiretsu* are Toyota and Honda. There are various tiers in vertical *kiretsu* with the lower tiers consisting of smaller manufacturers and suppliers (Figure 67).

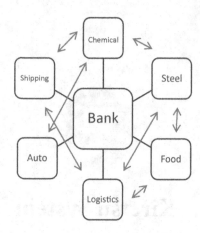

Figure 66: Classical *Kiretsu*

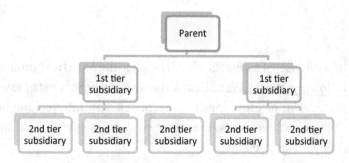

Figure 67: Vertical *Kiretsu*

Recent studies on *kiretsu* in the automobile industries suggest that car makers which bypass their traditional intermediary partners in the supply chains and deal directly with upstream parts manufacturers were able to generate more revenues due to reduction time and manufacturing costs (Matous & Yasuyiki, 2015). In today's competitive global environment, *kiretsu* may have to review their traditional supply chain structure or even develop new links with companies outside the grouping.

Case of Panasonic

Panasonic Corporation recorded a staggering loss of JPY780 billion (USD10.2 billion) in 2012. The company's president, Kazuhiro Tsuga, nicknamed Samurai CEO, had to take some radical measures to save the company. Panasonic was founded in 1918 and formerly known as Matsushita.

A Master of Science graduate from University of California, Santa Barbara, Kazuhiro Tsuga is willing to adopt certain Western management techniques to solve Panasonic's problems. He reduced the size of his management team from 30 to 10; cut staff at the Osaka headquarters from 7,000 to 130; cut managers' bonus by 35%, including his own pay cut of 60 percent; stripped 35 executives of their cars and drivers; and suspended quarterly dividends. Businesses that failed to make more than 5 percent profit had to be improved or exited. He reorganised the group's 468 subsidiaries and 94 associate companies into five major divisions — Business to Business (B2B) solutions, consumer electronics, automotive, housing and devices.

The company returned to the black in 2014 with a profit of JPY 120.4 billion (USD1.2 billion). Kazuhiro Tsuga is especially optimistic of the automotive division. The company has signed a partnership with electric-car maker Tesla to build and operate a USD5 billion lithium-ion battery facility in the Nevada desert outside Reno.

Kazuhiro Tsuga stressed that he does not believe in just reading reports of executives or headquarters (HQ). He needs to feel the pulse of the business on the ground. One way is to interact directly with customers or employees. This walking the ground approach gives him the opportunity to make changes to the company's products, if necessary.

Another change that Kazuhiro Tsuga had brought to Panasonic is the localisation of top management for Panasonic's operations worldwide. For example, its top executives in India are Indians, and they are supported by a team of Japanese executives. Similarly, Panasonic Avionics Corporation in California is managed by an American.

While Kazuhiro Tsuga has led Panasonic out of the doldrums, the business environment remains highly competitive for the company's five divisions. To sustain growth, it is imperative for senior management to not just think outside the box, but to change the shape of the box as well. This involves setting new industry standards or benchmarks for the various divisions. As such, each division should aim to be the business leader in the particular segment. The company should also foster collaboration with customers to gather customers' feedback on the features that they wish to see in its products (Figure 68).

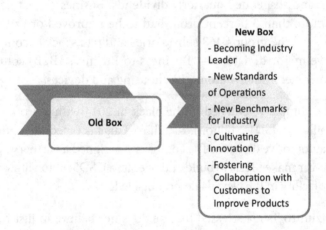

Figure 68: Changing the Shape of the Box

Chapter

35

Influences of Western Management Styles

The concept of *amae* (dependence and mutual dependence) still predominates in many Japanese organisations. The influence of Confucianism is manifested in the interpersonal relations between employees in different hierarchies in the organisation. The senior employee plays the role of *oyabun* (father) to the *kobun* (children). The *oyabun* is expected to look after the interests of *kobun*. In return, the *kobuns* have to show respect to the *oyabun*.

Many Japanese managers are incorporating Western management practices into their companies. These may involve strategic planning or merit-based promotion systems. In the traditional Japanese management system, the contribution of each member is indistinguishable from the team. The exposure to Western culture and management practices prompted many younger Japanese workers to seek self-identity and better recognition of their efforts. As such, they are impatient and do not favour *nenko joretsu* or seniority-based promotion system.

Companies in Japan are facing the predicament of having to offer lifetime employment and attracting highly motivated yet impatient executives. Under the lifetime employment seniority-based system, employees are promoted according to the number of years they spend with the company. This means that capable younger employees may not have the opportunity to rise up the corporate ladder within their desired time frame. At the same time, they may also not be adequately compensated for their individual efforts as many companies still emphasise team efforts. To address this situation, it may be worthwhile for senior management to put in place a reward system which recognises outstanding employees, in addition to the group contribution efforts.

The *ringi* consensus management system is often compared to Western participative management system. The former is more time-consuming as it requires consensus building and negotiations before a formal decision can be made. In most Japanese companies, important decisions are first made behind the scenes by the Chief Executive and his *jitsuryoku-sha* (kingmaker). This practice frustrates some executives who claimed that their views were not taken into consideration as top management had already made a decision in the first place. As the Chief Executive wields much power in the organisation, decision-making is in actual fact top-down rather than bottom-up. With changes in the marketplace, it is inevitable that top management need to change their approach when dealing with lower level subordinates. They have to adopt a more open approach to improve communication within the corporate setting and show that they are sincere in valuing the participation of employees.

Due to the changing business environment, Japanese managers are also feeling the pressure to outperform each other as competition between employees of equal ranks is becoming a norm. As such, managers may not be able to give appropriate advice to their subordinates. Individual performance-based system is catching-up as companies push for greater productivity of its workers. The emphasis on merit is slowly changing the traditional preference for collectivism in the workforce.

Business leaders are also feeling the pressure to raise stock prices and generate higher returns on investment. In response to these goals, managers are paying more attention to strategic planning rather than operational management. This shift of focus requires management to relook at new business paradigms to stay competitive.

In Japan, unions generally have a close relationship with management. This is because many senior managers have moved up through union ranks and serve as union officials. Union membership is open to managers up to the section chief level. Major Japanese corporations have done away with independent trade unions and replace them with a system of enterprise unionism. An enterprise union is a company union and not an industry-wide union. Enterprise union memberships are only limited to permanent employees, and not contract or temporary employees. Unions emphasise cooperation with management and promote team approach. This is unlike unions in the United States which are national unions and not company-based. As such, unions in the West are seen as adversaries to management.

Japanese companies are finding it increasingly difficult to recruit good employees. In addition to automating some job functions to increase productivity, they are also adopting new management styles to retain employees and to boost their productivity. Itochu Corporation, for example, introduced "morning-focused work style" with the aim of raising productivity for female employees who are unable to work through late nights. The company pays female employees extra wages for early morning work between 5 am and 8 am and provides meals. This is a case of *sampo yoshi* (satisfaction of three parties): employees, company and society.

The Japanese insurance industry is seeing a wave of work-style reforms. Nippon Life Insurance Company is converting 6,000 part-time clerical staff into employees with indefinite contracts. Fukoku Mutual Life Insurance Company also announced that it is giving 400 non-regular staff regular status. Workers with the new status have the opportunity to be promoted to deputy departmental chief. Another insurance company, Meiji Yasuda Life Insurance Company, made public that it will raise the retirement age for its employees to 65 from 2019.

Japan's Keidanren (Business Federation) has noted that future job seekers should possess a broad knowledge of liberal arts, humanities and sciences along with foreign language communication skills. Workers need to be able to act as independent individuals. They also need to respect diversity, accept the differences of others and collaborate with them. The three core concepts for human resource development that Keidanren has advocated are *Independence*, *Collaboration* and *Creation* (Figure 69).

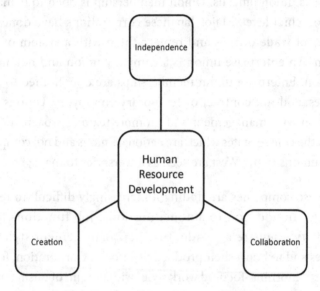

Figure 69: New Concept of Human Resource Development

Traditional Japanese management styles have many problems as the global economies change. While the bottom-up planning approach is popular among Japanese companies, important decisions are still done in a top-down manner.

In the case of Toyota Motors, the centralised top-down management style has slowed responses to consumers' complaints considerably. This management style has been criticised for being too parochial for a global company. The company has undergone some management shake-ups by recruiting non-Japanese CEOs for its U.S., African and Latin American operations.

Toyota's smaller rival, Honda Motors, adopted a more bottom-up approach by encouraging employees to solve problems through debate, regardless of rank, a practice known as *waigaya*. Its workers are expected to acquire knowledge by participating in each step of the production process, a practice described as *sangen shugi*. The company encourages individualism and is willing to recruit employees from different backgrounds. However, decision-making is still characterised by the *ringi* system. As such, both individual freedom and team cohesion are given equal priority in the company.

Table 4 lists some of the main problems with traditional management system.

Table 4: Problems of Traditional Japanese Management System

Management Practices	Problems
Ringi	This practice is time-consuming. Very often, decision has been made by top management. The signing on *rinsei* document or *ringi-sho* is just a formality. The competitive business environment demands decisions to be made rapidly. Companies which could not make decisions in the shortest possible time may lose their competitiveness in the marketplace.
Jitsuryoku-sha	These are people closely associated with the CEO or top management. They belong to his "inner-circle". Major important decisions are decided by the CEO and *jitsuryoku-sha* executives. The bottom-up decision-making approach may not be really effective as it has to pass through many layers before reaching top management.
Lifetime employment and seniority-based promotion	This encourages complacency among older employees as they know that their seniority and promotion are dependent on the length of time they work in the company. Those who are not totally efficient in their work and who do not contribute much may also be promoted to a higher level based on their number of years of service. The concept of *sekentei* (social conformity) discourages managers from moving to other companies. This practice demotivates younger employees as they feel that their efforts may not be recognised by the company.

(Continued)

Table 4: (*Continued*)

Management Practices	Problems
Job rotation	Employees are rotated across various departments. They become generalist instead of specialist and may not have the in-depth knowledge to resolve a particular problem.
Team reward	Team reward discourages the individual from putting in his best efforts as he knows that his contribution will not be acknowledged at an individual level but at a group level. He may feel that there is no need to do his best in his work.
Team concept	The team concept discourages individuals from becoming "superstar". Due to the homogeneity of the members of the team, individuals may not have the opportunity to realise their full potential.
Union members who are also managers	Since many union members are also managers, they may not fully serve the members' interests.
Bottom-up planning	Bottom-up planning takes time and the plan may not be fully supported by top management. If this is the case, much time and efforts are wasted.
In-house hiring of managers	In-house hiring precludes new talents from joining the company. As such, companies may not be able to fully aware of the new innovations out in the marketplace or incapable of upgrading their products to compete with their rivals.

Expatriates made up some of the highest paid executives in Japan in 2015. The top spot was held by Nikesh Arora of SoftBank Group Corp. with JPY8 billion (USD76 million). In the second spot was Joseph DePinto of Seven & I Holdings with JPY2.2 billion (Table 5).

The Japanese government introduced new regulations to boost corporate governance and increase board diversity. It also recommended that senior executives' compensation be tied to long-term returns of the company.

Table 5: Best Paid Executives

Company	Executive	2015 Compensation, Yen, Million	Nationality
SoftBank Group	Nikesh Arora	8,042	India
Seven & I Holdings	Joseph DePinto	2,187	United States
SoftBank Group	Ronald Fisher	2,096	United States
Nissan Motors	Carlos Ghosn	1,071	Brazil
Takeda Pharmaceutical	Christophe Weber	905	France
Hitachi Data Systems	Jack Domme	900	United States
Toyota Motors	Didier Leroy	696	France
Fanuc	Yoshiharu Inaba	690	Japan
Sony	Kazuo Hirai	513	Japan

Source: Bloomberg.

Case of Shiseido

Shiseido is a multinational company specialising in skin care, cosmetics, hair care and fragrance products. The company operates in over 120 countries. Its CEO, Masahiko Uotani, is a Masters in Business Administration graduate from the Columbia Business School. He is also the former chief of Coca-Cola Japan. He is the first Shiseido president to be appointed outside the company since it was founded in 1872.

Masahiko Uotani aimed to transform Shiseido into a leading global brand. Unlike most Japanese companies which focus on internal staff transfers and promotions, Shiseido is open to recruiting outsiders, specifically for their knowledge and expertise. Masahiko Uotani believes that diversity helps the company to "Think Globally, and Act Locally".

Shiseido is not just selling products. It is also selling emotional value. Masahiko Uotani said:

"Customers who buy the company's products should look and feel nice, both externally and internally."

Masahiko Uotani believes in creating customers' experience through luxurious stores before they consider purchasing the products online. As such, the company places great emphasis in generating customers' satisfaction of its products.

To position as a global brand, Shiseido added U.S. brands Nars, Laura Mercier and Bare Minerals, and French brands Avene and ReVive.

Shiseido needs to continue to come up with innovative strategies to build its brand equity if it wishes to remain as a global brand and to increase its market share. Figure 70 shows the main components of improving brand equity.

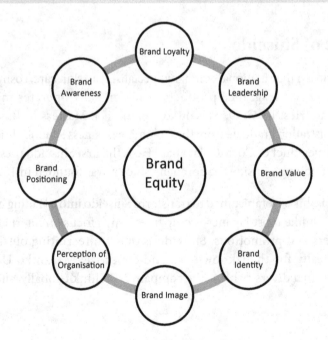

Figure 70: Components of Brand Equity

Case of Uniqlo

Uniqlo is one of Japan's largest casual wear designer, manufacturer and retailer. The company is owned by Fast Retailing. Currently operating in 17 countries with a total of 1,734 stores, Uniqlo hopes to overtake Gap, H&M and Zara as the world's largest apparel maker. Growth for the company comes mainly from Asia, followed by Europe and the United States.

The company's founder, Tadashi Yanai, is Japan's richest man with an estimated net worth of USD15 billion. Tadashi Yanai stressed that globalisation of Uniqlo has been his plan from the very beginning. One of the values which he follows is learning from failure. The failure of his stores in the United Kingdom in the early years did not stopped his efforts of focusing in that country.

Tadashi Yanai has constantly stressed that a company's goal and employees' dream should be in sync. In that way, employees will be more motivated to achieve the company's goal. The company has recently hired Christophe Lemaire, formerly from Hermes and Lacoste, to head its Paris research centre. Christophe Lemaire will be creating an entirely new line called Uniqlo U.

Uniqlo has signed on world number one tennis star Novak Djokovic and fifth seed Kei Nishikori as its brand ambassadors. Australian golfer Adam Scott has also come on-board as a Uniqlo ambassador. These are important breakthroughs for Uniqlo as it penetrates the sports apparel market. The company also hopes to identify suitable female athletes as its brand ambassadors as it aims to provide comfortable clothing suitable for all lifestyles.

Uniqlo has its share of controversies. The company was accused of failing to improve working conditions in its China's factories. Workers were abused to work overtime beyond legal limits and local thugs were called in to stop workers' protest. Its Guangzhou factory was reported to have discharged toxic chemicals into the sewage system.

In Japan, Uniqlo had announced that it will allow employees to take three days off in a week to promote work-life balance. Employees can choose to work 10 hours per day for 4 days instead of eight hours for five days. However, they have to work on weekends and public holidays.

This move to offer more working flexibility arrangement stems from the pressure of recruiting and retaining employees as Uniqlo seeks to increase its full-time local employees from 10,000 to 16,000.

As Uniqlo expands internationally, it has to balance planning with flexibility and to adapt to the different socio-cultural factors in the various countries. It has to meet the expectations of the country's workforce as well as that of its customers. Communicating its plans and intentions to its workforce while remaining flexible in order to respond to their changing needs will be a key factor determining the success of the company internationally (Figure 71).

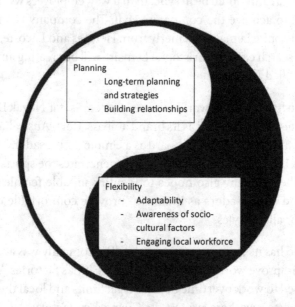

Planning
- Long-term planning and strategies
- Building relationships

Flexibility
- Adaptability
- Awareness of socio-cultural factors
- Engaging local workforce

Figure 71: Balancing Planning and Flexibility

Section 6

Korean Management Styles

36

Korean Philosophy and Religions

Korean philosophy is influenced mainly by Korean Shamanism, Buddhism, Confucianism and Daoism. In Shamanism, the shaman (mudang) seeks to interact with a spiritual world as he believes in the presence of three spirits: Sanshin (the Mountain Spirit), Toksong (the Recluse), and the Chilsong (the Spirit of the Seven Stars, the Big Dipper).

Buddhism was introduced from China during the Three Kingdoms period (57 B.C. to A.D. 668). Korean Buddhism was influenced by many of the beliefs of Shamanism as Koreans saw that Chinese Mahayana Buddhism was unable to resolve many internal inconsistencies. In the seventh and eighth centuries, the Seon school of Buddhism gained popularity. However, it was suppressed during the Joseon Dynasty (Chosun: 1392–1910) when Neo-Confucianism became widely practised.

Confucianism was also introduced to Korea during the Three Kingdoms period through ancient cultural exchanges between China and Korea. It flourished during the Joseon Dynasty under the guidance of Yi Hwang (Taegye) and Yi I (Yulgok). Today, it remains a fundamental part of

Korean society, influencing the moral values and social relations of many Koreans today.

Daoism arrived in Korea during the late Three Kingdoms period in A.D. 674. It was popularised during the Goryeo Dynasty but it remains a minor religious philosophy in Korea today.

During the period of Japanese colonial rule, from 1910 to 1945, Shintoism became the official religion in Korea. With the end of the war in 1945, the Shinto system was dismantled and disassociated from the state.

Chapter

37

Korean Management Practices

Much of Korean management style is similar to that of the Japanese as both have been largely influenced by Confucian ideology. Historically, Korea was a colony of Japan from 1910 to 1945. The two countries share common cultural heritage of Confucianism and Buddhism. Confucianism places great emphasis on politeness, humility, obedience and subordination. It reinforces the hierarchical, authoritarian and paternalistic corporate culture in Korea. The organisational structure is highly centralised with authority concentrated at top levels of management (Chen, 2004; Cho and Yoon, 2001). The company is portrayed as one big happy family with the CEO or President playing the role of a patriarch or father.

Korean management approach is hierarchical and paternalistic. Hofstede had classified South Korea as a country with relatively high power distance index (60). This means that Korean culture supports hierarchy and differentiates individuals based on seniority and social status. Managers are required to ensure that the team is cohesive and that members have good working relationships with each other. This is the concept of *inwha* or harmony among members of equal ranks. It is the duty of managers to take a holistic interest in their subordinates. In return, subordinates are expected to be loyal and obedient to their managers. Korean employees are considered to be even more loyal to their companies than Japanese employees (Choi & Nakano, 2008).

Like the Japanese, Korean managers look to consensus building when it comes to decision-making. This ensures that there are shared responsibilities among those who influence the outcome of a particular decision. Confucianism teaches that group needs are more important than personal needs. This is a philosophy that is widely accepted in Korean business world. This *collectivistic* nature also relates to networking and relationship building in the country. The corporate culture is highlighted in the company's *sahoon*. A *sahoon* reflects a company's vision, mission, core values and beliefs. It serves as a guide for management and employees to follow.

Koreans' relationship building is similar to Chinese *guanxi*. First, there is *inmaek*, which is social network in general. Then, there is *yongo*, which are relations based on family ties, university or schools, and place of origin. Finally, there is *yonjul*, which are relations developed for personal gains and benefits. People who went to the same school or college share a special relationship. The *sonbae* (senior) and *hoobae* (junior) relationship is similar to the Chinese *qianbei* and *houbei*, and Japanese *senpai* and *kohai* relationships.

Koreans, however, are more open to Western management styles, probably a result of the internationalisation of *chaebols* or conglomerates overseas. The new generation of Koreans are increasingly adopting the Western work culture, demanding more work-life balance and seeking self-fulfilment in their work. Korean employees generally adopt a more compromising style than Western counterparts (Kirkbride *et al.*, 1991). However, recent studies on U.S. employees have shown that U.S. managers also prefer less confrontational style as they become more exposed to globalisation and interacting with their counterparts from other countries (Paul *et al.* 2004).

To compete in the fast changing marketplace, Korean companies need to revamp their business processes. This involves revamping the hierarchical structure to a flatter structure to encourage freer communication. At the same time, the employee evaluation system should be based on performance rather than seniority.

Korean managers need to keep an open dialogue with unions as employees become more outspoken. They have to keep employees informed with up-to-date information regarding labour issues to minimise any serious problems with unions.

Hyundai Motor's labour disputes which loom year after year were due to the breakdown of wage negotiations with management. Hyundai's labour union had constantly protested about the army-style corporate culture and the priority given to technology over employees. However, in the light of worsening business conditions, both management and workers of Hyundai Motor agreed to a less generous wage package, at the time of writing.

Korea was able to weathered the storms of the 1997 Asian Financial Crisis and the 2008 Global Financial Crisis more effectively than Japan (Rowley & Jun, 2013). Two main reasons contributed to Japan's vulnerability to external shocks. The first was that over 90 percent of Japan's exports consisted of highly income elastic industrial supplies, capital goods and consumer durables. The collapse of the U.S. and European markets had a severe negative impact on Japan's exports. The second reason was the increasing proportion of exports to gross domestic product (GDP) ratio since the early 2000s. This was induced by the real effective exchange rate of the yen which finally returned to a level consistent with long-term average.

Chaebols are learning from the success of Japanese multinationals overseas. They face the same competitive pressure as their Japanese counterparts in international markets and learn to imitate the good practices of the Japanese. As such, they develop management styles which are somewhat similar to the Japanese. However, Korean companies are more successful in fostering a family atmosphere in which employees interact with managers. Korean employees normally attend "family meetings" at least once a month to discuss issues related to their work.

Table 6 shows the convergence of Korean and Japanese management styles.

Table 6: Korean and Japanese Management Styles

Factors of Growth	Korean	Japanese
Market share	More emphasis on market share than Japanese	Focus on market share
Technology development	Develop economies of scale with technology	Focus on flexible manufacturing and adaptation to changes in market
Supplier	Cooperate with suppliers in product development	Cooperate with suppliers in product development
Marketing	Focus on branding	Focus on branding
Human resource management	Convergence with Japanese style as firms internationalise. Korean companies are more willing to adopt Western style of management compared to Japanese companies. Less willing to consider employees' suggestions	Sharing of information and employees' suggestions

Korea has developed its own human resource policies and practices (Rowley & Bae, 2013). As its citizens become more educated and internationalised, the traditional human resource management practices have also undergone numerous changes. Traditionally, Korean human resource management is characterised by seniority-based practices and lifetime employment, similar to Japanese. However, Koreans are also more open to adopting performance-based human resource management system which is widely practised in the West. As such, there is the coexistence of two paradigms, the traditional and modern (Jeong, 2000).

There is a strong correlation between human resource system and firm performance in Korea (Bae and Lawler, 2000). The Korean form of performance management system is different from the U.S due to the unique social and cultural contexts in Korea. It contains various aspects of both traditional and modern systems.

Korean companies have also changed their recruitment strategies from mass recruitment of university graduates to recruitment based on demand. They are also more selective in their recruitment, preferring candidates with special skills than new graduates. This has also resulted in higher unemployment rates among Korean youths. According to government figures, about 500,000 young people enter the job market every year. Of this figure, 60 percent are degree holders. On the demand side, there are about 200,000 permanent positions available. The unemployment rate of Korean youths is around 9.5 percent currently. The keen competition for jobs in *chaebols* was evident when 100,000 applicants sat for entrance exams organised by Hyundai Corporation which offered 4,000 new positions in 2015.

Table 7 shows a comparison between Korean and Japanese human resource management system. There are many similarities between the two systems due to the common ideologies of Confucianism and Buddhism and due to the historical domination of Japan in Korea during the War. The major difference lies in the decision making approach between the two cultures. Human resource managers should consider the culture of their organisation when implementing human resource policies as each organisation has its own unique features (Lee and Lee, 2015).

Table 7: Korean and Japanese Human Resource Management System

Characteristics	Korean	Japanese
Criteria	Prefer new graduates	Prefer new graduates
Job assignments	After training and indoctrination, they are assigned to functional departments such as planning, finance or accounting. Family members, well-connected and elite groups are assigned to more important divisions.	Normally, assign to floor or field site first
Training and education	Non-systematic	Job rotation

(Continued)

Table 7: (*Continued*)

Characteristics	Korean	Japanese
Job rotation	Ad hoc	Regular
Evaluation	Non-systematic. However, performance management becoming more widespread.	Continuous
Promotion	Seniority	Seniority
Incentive system	Seasonal bonus	Performance-based incentive
Welfare	No	Yes
Retirement	At 55	Between 55–60
Mobility	Some mobility	Lesser mobility
Decision-making	Centralised decision structure. Top-down approach.	Bottom-up. Initiated by lower level employees.

Chapter

38

Chaebols

*C*haebols are business conglomerates with huge international operations. They are controlled by powerful families and assisted by government financing. *Chaebols* have played a major role shaping Korean economy since the 1960s. The model is similar to the Japanese Zaibatsu system. Among the well-known chaebols are Samsung, Hyundai, SK, LG, Lotte and Hanjin.

The listed units of Korea's top 10 *chaebols* accounted for over 50 percent of Korea's stock market capitalisation. In total, there were 181 listed companies of the 10 largest *chaebols*, with a combined market capitalisation of KRW778.5 trillion as of end July, 2016. Figure 72 shows the percentage market capitalisation of the top 10 conglomerates as of end July, 2016.

An important aspect of Korean business culture is "blood-based succession". The eldest son is normally the heir apparent and his relationship with his siblings is that of a father to the family (Chung *et al.*, 1997). The ownership of the business should be kept within the family (Kenna & Sondra, 1995).

Figure 72: Market Capitalisation

Source: The Korea Herald.

Chaebols have also received negative publicity in recent years. The failure of Daewoo Motors in 2000, the family feud at Doosan in 2005, the indictment of Samsung's chairman Lee Kun-Hee in 2008, the "nut rage" saga of Korean Air (part of the Hanjin Group) heiress Cho Hyun-ah in 2014, and the recent arrest of the sister of Lotte Group's chairman on bribery and embezzlement charges prompted calls for more restructuring and corporate governance of *chaebols*. Koreans are becoming increasingly disenchanted with the families of *chaebols* and resented their abuses and corrupt practices. Many would like to see the family structure dismantled and management put in the hands of capable managers rather than incompetent family members.

The younger generation of *chaebol* founding families have been the targets of public outrage due to their abuses of employees. The "prince and princess syndrome" run deep in younger generations of *chaebol* owner families as they have gained wealth without much efforts of their own. For example, much negative publicity had been generated when a third-generation of the Daelim Group, Lee Hae Wook, demanded that his chauffeur drive without the use of rear-view mirror citing the reason that their eyes should not meet in the mirror's reflection. This has caused many near collisions of his vehicle. In another instance, Chey Cheol Won of the SK Group, beat an employee with an aluminium baseball bat as other executives stood watching. The employee was protesting after being retrenched from an affiliate company. Chey Cheol Won threw USD1000 at the man for each strike he inflicted on the victim,

Case of Hanjin Shipping

The appointment of an incompetent person to head one of the largest shipping *chaebols*, Hanjin Shipping, has contributed to the financial woes of the company. Hanjin Group which is Korea's 10th largest *chaebol* also owns Korean Air. The group was founded by Cho Choong Hoon in 1945. His second son, Choi Soo-ho, managed the company until his death in 2006. Subsequently, his wife, Choi Eun Yang, took over the rein despite having no experience in the shipping industry. Hanjin Shipping has recently filed for court protection in 43 jurisdictions after creditors rejected its plan to restructure its massive debt of USD5.37 billion.

Korean banks have learnt from the collapse of the Daewoo Group, once Korea's second largest *chaebol*, in 1999. The myth that *chaebols* are "too big to fail" no longer holds true. Banks are now more prudent in their lending. In the case of Hanjin Shipping, its lead creditor, Korea Development Bank, said that inadequate support from parent Hanjin Group to an ongoing debt restructuring plan prompted other creditor banks to pull the plug.

which he later raised to USD3,000. Such *gabjil* or high-handedness by *chaebol* scions prompted calls to set up legislations to punish those who committed serious abuses.

At the time of writing, Korea is swarmed with negative news of wrongdoings of *chaebol* family members. Table 8 is a small compilation of wrongdoings reported in various press articles.

The Global Competitiveness Report by the World Economic Forum ranked South Korea 37th in the World Corruption Perceptions Index and 123rd in transparency in public policymaking. In another report by Transparency International, a Berlin-based organisation, South Korea was ranked 27th in 2015 among 34 members of the Organisation for Economic Co-operation and Development (OECD) countries in its Perceived Corruption Index.

Table 8: Alleged Wrongdoings of *Chaebol* Family Members

Chaebol Family Members	Alleged Wrongdoings
Samsung chairman Lee Khun-Hee	Paying women for illegal sexual services
Hyosung chairman's son Cho Hyun-Joon	Embezzlement and breach of trust
CJ chairman Lee Jay-Hyun	Embezzlement, breach of trust, and tax evasion
Lotte founder Shin Kyuk-Ho and son Shin Dong-Bin	Embezzlement and breach of trust
Lotte Foundation chief Shin Jung-Ya	Embezzlement and bribery
SK vice chairman Chey Jae-Won	Embezzlement (recently paroled)
Orion chairman Tam Chul-Kon	Embezzlement (currently, embroil in lawsuit brought about by former executives for forcing them to commit perjury)

To combat graft, the government introduced a tough anti-corruption law which took effect on September 28, 2016. The law covers some 4 million civil servants and employees of educational institutions. They are banned from accepting gifts worth KRW50,000 (USD45) or more. Businesses fear that placing a limit on accepting dinners and gifts could further dampen the sluggish domestic consumption. The economic growth of 2016 at 2.7 percent is only moderately higher than the 2.6 percent recorded in 2015.

The inter-dependence between *chaebols* and the government in power was evident in many cases where convicted tycoons were pardoned by former Korean Presidents. For example, the chairmen of Samsung, Lee Kyun-Hee, Hyundai Motor's Chung Mong-Koo, and Hanwha's Kim Seung-Youn were all pardoned by President Lee Myung-Bak for their previous convictions. *Chaebols* wield considerable influence over government policies as many bureaucrats and judges see *chaebols* as ideal organisations to work for after retirement from government service. As such, they would not want to be overly critical of the tycoons' wrongdoings. This is somewhat similar to the *amakudari* system in Japan.

Chaebols have also been blamed for aggravating the large income disparity between the higher-income and lower-income groups. Various political parties have called for the curbing of power of the *chaebols* in order to give small and medium-sized enterprises greater chances of survival. A recent report by research firm Chaebul.com found that despite the growth in assets and revenues of the top five *chaebols* between 2013 and 2015, their contribution to job growth remained at 57.7 percent out of the total top 30 conglomerates.

Case of SK Group

SK Group is one of Korea's largest *chaebols* with businesses in the telecommunications, IT services, chemicals, construction of plants, and infrastructure products sectors.

Its chairman Chey Tae-Won was reinstated in 2016 after serving almost three years in prison for embezzlement. Chey Tae-Won was pardoned by President Park Geun-Hye along with thousands of other business leaders citing that they are needed to help lift South Korea's economy. While some shareholders objected to his reinstatement, there was little they could do as Chey Tae-Won and his family and business associates own close to half of the company's shares.

The close shareholding structure of *chaebols* prompted much criticism that company boards lack independence and suffer from poor corporate governance. This, in turn, discourages foreign investments into South Korea.

SK Group is identifying new markets for growth as the local market is quite saturated. It is counting on SK Innovation, SK Telecom and SK Hynix to spearhead the Group's growth.

SK Group could mitigate negative publicity if it could push for more changes within the organisation. It should rebuild public trust and confidence and reduce the negative perception of the company.

The company should introduce certain policy changes to review the behaviours of employees who are not aligned with the proper conduct demanded by the organisation. It is thus essential for senior management to lead the change by managing stability. Stability provides the machinery for the day-to-day operation of the business. At the same time, managing change ensures the transformation process is on the right track towards something better (Figure 73).

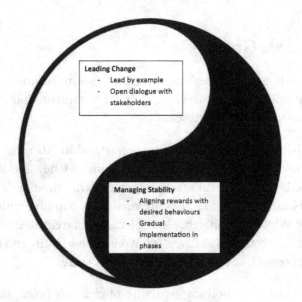

Figure 73: Balance between Leading Change and Managing Stability

Chaebols' expansion overseas has resulted in many conflicts between Korean managers and host countries' workers who are having difficulties adapting to the Korean style of management. Different communication styles or value systems often lead to tensions and divergent viewpoints (Beebee & Mottet, 2010). Korean managers who are based overseas need to understand the fundamental cultural differences between themselves and employees of different nationalities. They need to be holistic in their management approach (Lim, 2009).

Korean managers operating in a foreign country need to understand the cultural differences between Korea and the host country. The failure or the inability to adapt to the host-country culture often gives rise to conflicts between Korean managers and employees (Tung, 1988). Hofstede (2001) noted that as leaders' values vary across cultures, they also need to be trained to understand the cross-cultural differences and adjust their leadership styles to perform successfully in different cultures.

Case of Amore Pacific

Amore Pacific is one of South Korea's leading cosmetic companies. It carries major brands such as Sulwhasoo, Laneige, Mamonde, Etude House and Innisfree. The company is currently run by Suh Kyung-Bae, a MBA graduate from Cornell University. Suh Kyung-Bae was named Businessman of the Year in 2015 by Forbes Asia. His fortune is estimated to be around USD10.7 billion. In 2015, Forbes ranked Amore Pacific 21st in its list of World's Most Innovative Companies.

Amore Pacific has defied Korea's reliance on electronics and information technology. It has successfully contributed to improving the country's brand competitiveness. Sales last year amounted to KRW4.7 trillion. It is currently the 14th largest cosmetic manufacturer in the world. Growth was bolstered by public interests in environmentally friendly products; the rising income of Chinese consumers; and the popularity of K-pop culture.

China accounted for over 50 percent of the group's total sales. Penetrating the Chinese market was no easy task as it took the company 20 years to understand its customers' taste and preferences. The company is also targeting Singapore as the next hub for growth in Southeast Asia. Suh Kyung-Bae's next challenge is to replicate China's success stories in the Middle East and Latin America. He has to devise strategies which bridge the concept of beauty across different cultures.

To ride on the popularity of K-pop stars, Amore Pacific has signed on popular actress Song Hye Kyo as brand ambassador for Laneige, and actor Lee Min Ho and Im Yoona of Girls Generation for Innisfree.

At Amore Pacific, employees address each other without their titles. Suh Kyung-Bae tries to break down the hierarchical structure and creates a more personalised working environment. Suh Kyung-Bae is also an unconventional boss as he personally tries all products, with the exception of mascara, before they are launched. To understand female customers better, he often seeks feedbacks from his wife, daughters and the company's female employees.

Suh Kyung-Bae believes it is essential for South Korea to be in the forefront of science and technology. The country has been a follower rather than a market leader of technological products for many years. Suh Kyung-Bae recently established a Science Foundation with his own money amounting to KRW300 billion (USD268 million) to conduct life sciences research and to encourage young scientists to venture into new areas.

To grow Amore Pacific's brands internationally, the company could adopt a multidimensional approach of brand luxuriousness. It has to understand how consumption of luxury brands is influenced by socio-cultural factors and experiences of consumers in those countries. Bian and Forsythe (2012) noted that affective attitudes are powerful predictors of behaviour as they involve consumers' feelings and emotions. Luxury brands also give the consumers some form of self-expression and fulfilment. Figure 74 illustrates a multidimensional approach to brand luxuriousness.

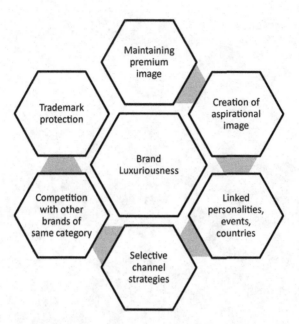

Figure 74: Multidimensional Approach of Brand Luxuriousness

Collaboration among Rivals

I n a joint venture, as the knowledge is transferred among partners, their capabilities become more similar. Each partner contributes its own strength and resources to the joint venture and complements the others (Nakamura, *et al.*, 1996).

However, the partners in a joint venture may be concerned about divulging too much intellectual property and trade secrets. Nicholls-Nixon and Woo (2003) noted that joint ventures where the technology is constantly changing develop fewer patents.

Case of Toshiba Samsung Storage Technology

Toshiba Samsung Storage Technology (TSST) is a joint venture established in 2004 between Toshiba Corporation (Japan) and Samsung Electronics Co. (Korea). Toshiba owns 51% of TSST with the balance 49% owned by Samsung Electronics Co. The company has two headquarters: Kawasaki, Japan and Suwon, Korea. Each company in Japan and Korea has its own board of directors. TSST is responsible for the product development, marketing and sales of Optical Disc Drives. TSST will tap on the existing networks of both Toshiba Corp. and Samsung Electronics Co. (Figure 75).

Figure 75: Toshiba Samsung Storage Technology

This joint venture is a win-win situation as there is no clash of Japanese and Korean cultures. In addition, the vast network of both Toshiba and Samsung's sales and service network provide great convenience to customers. The motivation for both companies include: efficiencies in branding, marketing and services; collaboration instead of competition; sharing of industry knowledge and access to greater resources including specialist staff and technology. With a common branding, the company is able to access a much larger market than if each party ventures out on its own (Figure 76).

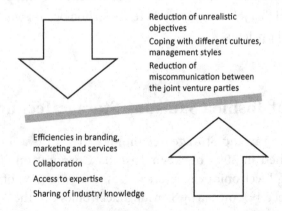

Figure 76: Advantage of Toshiba Samsung Joint Venture

At the same time, by having two corporate headquarters and two separate boards, the joint venture reduces the problems of cultural integration and differences in objectives from both parties.

Case of Hitachi and LG Data Storage

A similar joint venture exists between Hitachi Ltd and LG Electronic Inc. The company has consistently maintained the number one position in the world optical storage market since 2001. It has a Japanese President for its Tokyo headquarter and a Korean President for its Seoul headquarter. Hitachi holds a majority stake in the joint venture. Hitachi will contribute its DVD-ROM/RAM drive technology while LG will contribute its CD-ROM and CD-RW drives technologies (Figure 77).

Through the joint venture, both companies are able to reduce procurement and development costs. At the same time, each company is able to leverage on the others' strength in technology development. There is a change in the structure of the media storage market as CD is replaced by DVD and read-only format is replaced by recordable/rewritable type. Hitachi could tap into the rewritable technology of LG while LG could also have access to Hitachi's DVD expertise.

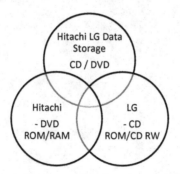

Figure 77: Hitachi LG Data Storage

Chapter

40

Korean Culture

One notable aspect of Korean culture is *kibun* or pride, dignity, or face. *Kibun* is a concept of Korean culture and social life and permeates every aspects of Korean society. It is directly related to pride, face or state of mind. Korean places great value to creating and maintaining an atmosphere of peace and harmony. In business, it is important not to hurt the *kibun* of another person. Managers have to avoid hurting the *kibun* of subordinates. Likewise, a manager's *kibun* is damaged if subordinates do not show proper respect to the manager. Foreigners have to be mindful of the subtleties in communication and maintain a harmonious atmosphere at all times, even if it means telling "white lies" to the Korean partners.

Closely associated to *kibun* is *nunchi*. It is the ability to identify another person's *kibun* by carefully observing the person's body language as well as the tone of his voice. *Nunchi* plays a crucial role in determining the success of a business negotiation. *Nunchi* is similar to the Western concept of emotional intelligence.

Yoyu is another important concept which refers to the inner strength and the ability to remain calm even in the most trying situations. A manager showing *yoyu* is one who demonstrates virtue and dignity. *Yoyu* could be traced back to the teachings of Confucius:

> *"The superior man thinks always of virtue.*
> *The common man thinks of comfort."*

Another valued characteristic of a successful manager is *jongsin*. It refers to perseverance, mental energy and fighting spirit. For decades, Koreans have been living in the shadows of the Japanese. Their high *jongsin* have enabled them to develop their own unique identity which is making waves globally as evidenced in the popularity of K-pop and K-drama.

Like Japanese, Korean managers develop business relationships from drinking at bars and salons. As Koreans rely heavily on non-verbal communication cues, getting drunk is one way to see the other person's true personality. Subordinates are expected to stay late till the night and send their drunk managers back home. Some Koreans regard a good drinker as more important than a good worker.

Koreans, like their Japanese counterparts, bow all the time. A short bow and head directed downwards suffice. It is noteworthy to follow certain etiquette when exchanging business cards. Folding or stuffing another person's business card into a pocket or wallet is faux pas. It pays to invest in a presentable business card holder.

Bringing small gifts to a business meeting is considered acceptable. However, business people should be aware that Korea has a reputation for corruption and that corruption charges brought against influential businessmen are quite common. The correct manner of receiving gifts is also important. The receiving hand should be held underneath by the non-receiving hand.

Case of SPC Group

SPC Group is one of South Korea's largest food and confectionary products with brands such as Paris Baguette, Paris Croissant, La Grillia, Caffe Pascucci and Jamba Juice. It also operates the Baskin Robbins, Dunkin' Donuts and Shake Shack Burger under franchise arrangement.

SPC is managed by Hur Young-In, an Economics graduate from Kyung Hee University. Hur Young-In learnt about bread-making at the American Institute of Baking in Kansas in 1981.

The group currently operates over 3,000 stores in South Korea, China, United States, Vietnam and Singapore. To penetrate the overseas market, Paris Baguette has localised its products to suit local palates. For example, in China the company has conducted extensive market research since the mid-1990s. Currently, it has over 120 stores in China.

Paris Baguette has successfully fused Western baking techniques with Asian flavours, introducing breads containing red beans, hot dogs, condensed milk, custards, etc. Offering varieties is another key differentiator of Paris Baguette. Currently, there are over 150 different items offered by the bakery chain.

Hur Young-In emphasises on teamwork as a key success factor for the company. Integration is a keyword at SPC. In his 2013 New Year Message, he stressed:

"We should gather wisdom through active communication and build overall capability with active interaction."

Hur Young-In plans to open at least 50 Paris Baguette stores in Singapore by 2020. The company will have to face stiff competition from more established local brands such as BreadTalk and Yakun Kaya Toast. It also plans to use Singapore as a base for its expansion into other Southeast Asian countries.

The penetration into Southeast Asian countries requires much market research as the region comprises many diverse cultures. The company not only has to deal with the diversities in local palates, but also diversities in workforce, language, business regulations, and social and cultural values (Figure 78).

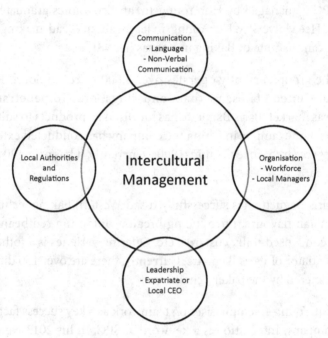

Figure 78: Management Dimensions of Culture

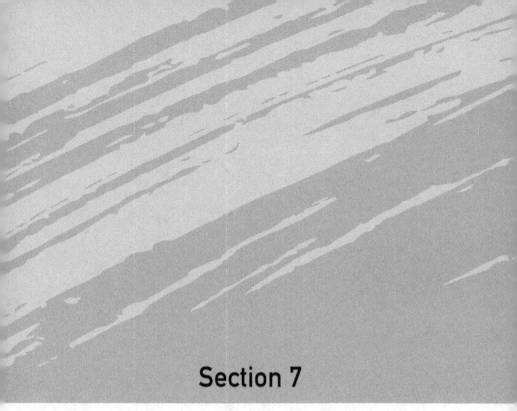

Section 7

Comparison of
Chinese, Japanese and Korean
Management Styles

Chapter

41

Differences in
Management Styles

This chapter compares and contrasts the management styles of Chinese, Japanese and Korean managers. Japanese and Korean management systems share some commonalities, although the degree or extent is not similar. These include consensual decision-making, lifetime employment, and paternalistic leadership. All three management styles also emphasize group harmony as a key element in their management philosophies.

The differences in cultures influence management styles and practices of managers even though there are common ideologies of Confucianism and Buddhism in them. Knowing a manager's decision-making style pattern, we could predict how a manager will react to various situations (Rowe & Boulgarides, 1994). Factors that influence decision makers are values and cognitive perception. Hofstede (1983b) noted that different people from different cultures exhibit different values. Nagashima (1993) found that Japanese show significant differences in cognitive perceptions from Westerners. Rowe and Boulgarides (1983) developed a decision style model that recognised the influences of values and cognitive perceptions on decision-making (Figure 79).

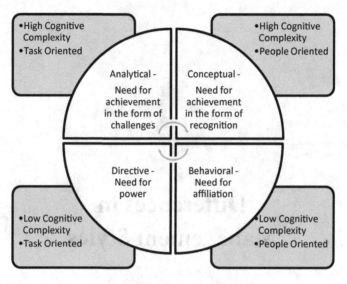

Figure 79: Decision Style Model

Martinsons (2001) found that American managers had the highest mean scores on "Analytical" and "Conceptual" decision styles. These could be explained by the prevalence of scientific management and dominance of Western management ideologies.

Chinese managers tend to have higher "Directive" decision style, reflecting the high power distance index and group collectivism. Decision-making is often centralised as Chinese managers seek social order through a well-defined hierarchical arrangement.

Japanese managers, on the other hand, display higher "Behavioral" decision style, suggesting the high degree of collective decision-making at the lower and middle management levels.

Given the above information, we could categorise the different decision styles of American, Chinese, Japanese and Korean managers in the Decision Style Model. As Korean management style is largely from a top-down approach, it is more similar to the paternalistic Chinese style than the bottom-up Japanese style. At the same time, Korean managers display more sharing of responsibilities when it comes to decision-making. Korean managers do not give praise easily as they feel that success should be shared by the group and not by any single individual. As such, there is an inclination towards affiliation to the group rather than individual achievements. This places Korean management style somewhere in between "Directive" and "Behavior" quadrant (Figure 80).

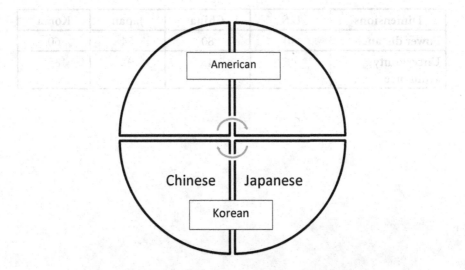

Figure 80: Decision Style of Oriental and American Managers

The differences in management styles between American and Oriental managers could be further elaborated through analysing the main functions of managers: Strategic Planning, Organising, Human Resource Managing, and Leading and Controlling.

Hofstede noted that United States has a low power distance index score of 40 while China has a high score of 80. Japan has a medium score of 54 and Korea has an intermediate score of 60.

In terms of uncertainty avoidance, the United States and China attain scores of 46 and 45, respectively. Americans tend to be more open to new ideas and willing to accept alternative opinions. For the Chinese, ambiguity is part of nature. This is reflected in the ideologies of Daoism where things are constantly changing but there is an overall balance of *Ying* and *Yang*.

Japan and Korea record uncertainty avoidance scores of 92 and 85, respectively. These show that Koreans and Japanese prefer to maintain rigid codes of beliefs and behaviours. They prefer the norms where things are predictable and may resist new ideas or innovations (Table 9).

Table 9: Scores on Hofstede's Cultural Dimensions

Dimensions	U.S.	China	Japan	Korea
Power distance	40	80	54	60
Uncertainty avoidance	46	45	92	85

Strategic Planning

American:

- By top management, communicated downwards, slow implementation process of projects
- Formal bureaucratic structure
- Reflect a high need for achievement, performance oriented
- Short-term goals, satisfy shareholders' requirements
- Low uncertainty avoidance, low power distance
- Based on formal explanatory model

Chinese:

- By top management, slow implementation process
- Formal bureaucratic structure
- Reflect a high need for power
- Both long- and short-term goals
- Low uncertainty avoidance, high power distance
- Based on experiential/empirical figures

Japanese:

- By participation of lower level employees, collective decision-making process
- Informal organisational structure/ organisational culture
- Reflect a high need for affiliation
- Fast implementation
- Long-term goals
- High uncertainty avoidance, prefer conformity, intermediate power distance
- Based on experiential/empirical figures

Korean:

- By top management, collective responsibilities of lower level managers
- Reflect a need for power yet a need for affiliation (in between Chinese and Japanese)
- Formal organisational structure
- Slower implementation, long-term goals
- High uncertainty avoidance, prefer conformity, intermediate power distance
- Based on experiential/empirical figures

Organising

American:

- Formal structures
- Individual responsibilities
- Identify with profession rather than firms

Chinese:

- Formal bureaucratic structure
- Mix of collective and individual responsibilities

Japanese:

- Informal organisational structure
- Collective responsibilities and accountability

Korean:

- Formal bureaucratic structure
- Collective responsibilities and accountability

Human Resource Managing

American:

- No job security
- Fast promotion depending on performance
- Minimal employee training and development
- Loyal to profession than firms

Chinese:

- Some job security
- Slow promotion, depending on seniority
- Some employee training and development
- Little loyalty to profession and firms

Japanese:

- High job security
- Slow promotion, depending on seniority
- High employee training and development, usually at site or floor
- High loyalty to profession and firms

Korean:

- Intermediate job security
- Slow promotion, depending on family ties and relations with management
- Performance management more widespread than Japanese
- High employee training and development, usually at headquarters
- High loyalty to firms

Leading and Controlling

American:

- Directive, top-down
- Confrontational
- Formal control rules and procedures
- "Blame" culture

Chinese:

- Directive, top-down
- Cooperation and harmony
- Manager exercises formal control
- Group and individual responsibilities
- "Saving face" rather than "blaming"

Japanese:

- Participative leadership, cooperation, bottom-up
- Group responsibilities
- "Saving face" rather than "blaming"

Korean:

- Directive, top-down
- Group responsibilities
- "Saving face" rather than "blaming"

Chapter

42

Core Values of Cultures

China, Japan and Korea share many cultural commonalities. They are all influenced by Confucianism and Buddhism. However, they are also different in many respects. Figure 81 compares the main characteristics of the business cultures of these three countries.

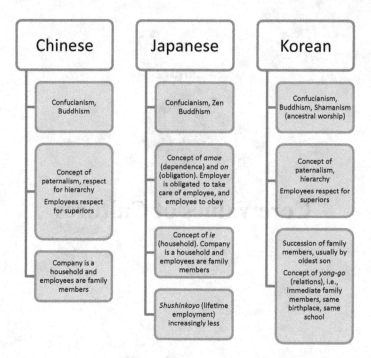

Figure 81: Overview of Corporate Cultures among Chinese, Japanese and Korean Firms

Case of IKEA in the East

IKEA Japan:

IKEA opened its first Japanese store in 2006. The company had spent more than five years planning and conducting market research before deciding to go on a large scale in Japan. To promote its products as suitable for small Japanese homes, IKEA set up outdoor showrooms around Tokyo. The size of these showrooms are equivalent to 4.5 tatami mats, and are thus called IKEA 4.5 Museums.

To achieve its planned expansion to 14 stores by 2020, IKEA actively engages local communities to understand about their needs. The company's vision "to create a better everyday life for the many people" means that it intends to be more than just a furniture company. Creating a better life does not just apply to its customers, but also its employees. IKEA's corporate culture embodies strong teamwork where everybody contributes to achieving the goal of the company. The company sees its employees as long-term working partners who are able to enjoy job security with permanent contracts. This concept is in line with the Japanese management system of teamwork, commitment and lifetime employment.

IKEA understands that most consumers come to its stores by public transport due to the heavy traffic in the cities. As such, it has introduced the "tebura de box" where customers could pack their small items into a box and have them delivered to their home for a fee.

IKEA Japan has also customised its products to fit the Japanese home. For example, sofas and beds have been made smaller so as not to take up additional living space. To whet the appetite of food lovers, IKEA recently introduced an all-black "ninja" hot dog that resembles a ninja scroll in Japan. The black colour is due to the addition of edible bamboo charcoal which is said to help detox the body or treat food poisoning. Such small move adds to the overall perception that IKEA is a fun and trendy place to go to for shopping and dining.

IKEA China:

IKEA entered the Chinese market in 1998. It formed a joint venture as it needed to comply with local laws and to give it time to understand the market. It currently operates 21 stores in China. Its products are perceived as more expensive than comparable Chinese products. As such, IKEA carries more made-in-China products to keep its costs low. Raw materials are sourced locally for its two factories in Shanghai to avoid high import taxes. Like Japan, most of IKEA's customers in China do not own cars. Hence, most of IKEA's stores are located in downtown areas or next to rail networks. It also offers home delivery and fee-based assembly services to its customers.

IKEA China currently has to deal with a growing problem in China — customers napping at IKEA stores to take refuge from the heat outside. Store management does not discourage shoppers from sleeping on furniture. While such practice is considered unacceptable in European countries, IKEA understands that Chinese are accustomed to sleeping in public. Perhaps, the company hopes that some of these shoppers who sleep in the stores would buy and become actual customers when they are convinced of the comfort of IKEA's furniture. This is important as IKEA adapts to the Chinese culture and fine-tunes its retailing strategies.

Unlike Japan, Chinese homes have become slightly larger as the population becomes more affluent. Chinese customers have become more willing to spend on furnishing to decorate their homes and look towards contemporary designer furniture. IKEA's products are seen as having relatively good quality and fit the aspirations of the young middle-class population. The company also has to customise its products based on local needs. For example, it has to make standard-sized beds for the Chinese markets, unlike those initially sold in Hong Kong which are slightly shorter. To reach out to a wider customer base, IKEA has aggressively used social media such as Weibo to promote its products. The company is also launching its e-commerce platform to offer its products online as it hopes to reach out to more customers in cities where it does not have physical stores.

IKEA China suffered damages to its reputation recently when it refused to recall almost 1.7 million chests and dressers which could pose a danger to children if not fixed properly to walls. It has to make an embarrassing reversal of its earlier decision as critics claimed that IKEA has set double safety standards, one for the West and another for China. While the company has tried to adapt to local market needs, the latest episode shows that there is much more it can do to improve its image as a socially responsible company.

IKEA Korea:

IKEA opened its largest store in the world in Gwangmyeong, less than an hour drive from Seoul in 2014. The store occupies more than 59,000 square metres of sales area and offers 8,600 products in its 65 showrooms. Its former country manager, Patricik Schuerpf, had spent considerable amount of time since 2008 to build up good relations with various Korean government agencies before the opening of the megastore.

IKEA's success in the country is attributed to the better reception of Koreans towards do-it-yourself products. Many customers see its products as relatively affordable as compared to local products. To keep its price competitive, delivery fees and assembly fees are optional.

Much efforts have been put into the Gwangmyeong store to show how European furniture can blend in with Korean homes. Its cafeteria also offers local gastronomy delights such as kimchi bibimbap and kimchi salmon rice in addition to its Swedish meatballs.

The Swedish giant has also created waves of innovation in the local furniture market. Local competitors have to innovate themselves in order to compete with IKEA. Korea's largest furniture maker, Hanssem, was forced to reduce its production costs through automation and standardisation of parts in addition to focusing on improving customers' service. Another competitor, Livart — Korea's second largest furniture company — stepped up its marketing efforts aimed at younger customers through online sales and expanding its range of product offerings.

As competition increases in the local market, Korean furniture manufacturers are looking overseas to expand their market base. ILOOM, a specialised home furniture unit of the Fursys Group, plans to enter the China market this year (2017), following its expansions into Taiwan and Hong Kong. At the same time, Hanssem is also gearing up to open its first store in Shanghai this year. The company also announced that it will operate an online mall to sell its home furnishings and kitchenware.

Cross Cultural Competency of IKEA

Cross cultural competency is complex and multifaceted. It comprises the elements of skills, knowledge and attitude (Figure 82). Achieving cultural competency is more complicated than just gaining cultural awareness (Abbe & Halpin, 2009). To be truly successful operating in a different culture, businesses have to understand the sources and manifestations of the particular culture.

In the case of IKEA, while it has invested much time and efforts into building relationships with governmental authorities and the communities, it still has much to improve in the area of attitude as evidenced in the recent case relating to the recall of unstable chests and drawers.

Skills relates to relationship building, communication and self-monitoring. *Attitude* includes cultural empathy, open mindedness and being sensitive to the feelings of the local communities. *Knowledge* covers cultural awareness of the various countries as well as having a global perspective.

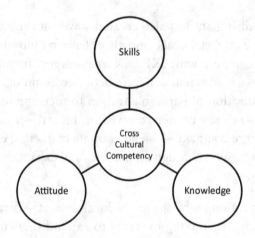

Figure 82: Cross Cultural Competency Model

Section 8

West Learning from the East

43

What Western Managers Could Learn from Their Eastern Counterparts?

So, what lessons could Western managers learn from their Oriental counterparts? Some Eastern management practices are more effective at resolving business problems than using Western management approach. Table 10 lists some Eastern theoretical foundations and management practices to solve common management problems facing Western managers.

Much of the daily problems of Western managers could be mitigated in Confucian-oriented working environment. Disagreements and conflicts are viewed from a harmony perspective in the Orient whereas they are viewed from a conflict perspective in the West. The author proposes a framework of conflict resolution using the Oriental management ideologies focusing on harmony and social values (Figure 83).

Western theories of leadership are based on empirical evidence while Oriental managers are strongly influenced by Confucian, Daoist and Buddhist

Table 10: Application of Oriental Management Practices to Solve Western Problems

Common Problems	Recommendations
Lack of teamwork in problem solving	Collectivism Group effort Collaboration Participation of team members
Conflict resolution	Compromising "Saving face" for all parties
Attitudes and behavioural issues	Advocate Confucianism teachings of harmony and respect for authority
Legal suit	Use *guanxi* or relationship to resolve differences
Production	Just-In-Time *Kaizen* (solving problems step-by-step)
Managerial miscommunication	Western managers take charge of project with little personal guidance from superiors, yet they are held accountable for the result of performance Eastern managers provide guidance and personal support to subordinates. This reduces miscommunication between managers and subordinates
Office relationships	Western managers feel that professional relationships should not get personal Oriental managers develop personal relationships which are useful to solve problems
Setting clear and measurable employee objectives	The paternalistic Oriental style of management calls for guidance of subordinates by superiors. This reduces differences in expectations between managers and subordinates
Low productivity	Small quality circles or work teams to identify, analyse and solve work-related problems could be introduced to resolve problems of low productivity

(Continued)

Table 10: (*Continued*)

Common Problems	Recommendations
Maintaining commitment	Creating a healthy organisational structure with proper reporting and accountability, coupled with guidance from senior managers. Involving subordinates in decision-making can get them to be more committed in the project and increase their sense of belonging. This is the concept of workplace as family and employees as family members

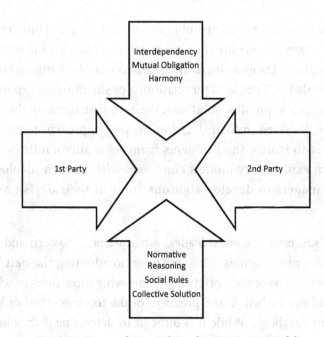

Figure 83: Proposed Oriental Conflict Resolution Model

ideologies. It is, therefore, advisable to adopt a fusion of Western and Oriental management styles to deal with challenges in the rapidly changing world.

Japanese and to a lesser degree, Koreans, make decisions by consensus. While this process takes much longer time to reach a decision, any decision made is supported by all those involved in the process. Thus, there are no major disagreements once the decision is made.

Japanese also look at problems from a different perspective. Rather than emphasising on answers to the problem, Japanese seek to define the question to the problem. They are focused on understanding the problem and consider all possible alternatives before reaching a final decision. And it is through this process that Japanese aim to achieve consensus. With such an approach without a preconceived answer in mind, Japanese are able to look at a problem with an unbiased mind. Westerners, on the other hand, base most of their decisions on empirical evidence and display biasness due to their predilections, beliefs and experiences (Yu, 2016).

Oriental managers accept ambiguity, uncertainty and imperfection as part of an organisation's life (Pascale & Athos, 1981). This is attributed to the philosophy of Daoism where things are constantly changing but there is an overall balance. They look for relationships surrounding problems with the aim of finding possible solutions. Western managers, on the contrary, are more rule-based in their decision-making approach, requiring facts and figures to isolate the problems from their surroundings. The use of Western explanatory models combined with Eastern ideologies will enable managers to develop rigorous rules in their decision-making process.

Many successful business leaders advocate both Eastern and Western management philosophies. They are open to adopting the best business practices regardless of their origins. The following three cases provide some background on the beliefs and practices of the top executives of Walmart, Airbnb and Facebook. While it is difficult to determine if they have been influenced by Eastern management philosophies, we could assume that their awareness of different cultures in those countries which they operate in is a key factor for their success in managing these global companies.

Case of Walmart's Walton Brothers

Walmart is the largest company in the world measured by sales revenue. It recorded USD482 billion in sales for the financial year end 2016, of which 26 percent came from international operations. It currently operates 11,500 stores under 63 banners in 28 countries and e-commerce sites in 11 countries.

Walmart was founded by Sam Walton in 1962. In 1992, his son, Robson Walton, took over the helm of the company. Robson Walton has a different style of management from his father. Senior Walton was an archetypal entrepreneur while Robson Walton preaches the humble servant leadership philosophy. He advocates listening to customers above everything else. Walmart's employees are called associates and there are 2.3 million associates worldwide.

His humbleness is evident from the size of his office which measures around 100 square feet. It is much smaller than most of his other senior executives and there are no windows. Another reflection of his servant leadership approach is shown in the 2016 company's annual report where he is seen standing near one end in the group photo of senior executives. His brother, Jim Walton, similarly chooses an obscure position standing behind a senior executive. This is unlike Asian bosses who always choose to be the centre of attention in any group photos.

Jim Walton, like his elder brother Robson, adopted the servant leadership management approach. Jim Walton is the chairman and CEO of Arvest Bank, which owns and operates 16 community banks in the United States. Like Walmart, Arvest Bank's employees are called associates. Jim Walton would assure that his associates receive everything that they need to serve the customers better. Such customer-oriented approach has made Arvest Bank a perennial favourite among customers in the Southwest region of the United States.

In its 2016 ranking of *The World's Billionaires*, Forbes ranked Jim Walton as the 15th richest man in the world with assets of

USD33.6 billion. His elder brother, Robson Walton, was ranked 17th with fortune of USD31.9 billion.

Under the servant-leadership model, both Robson and Jim have considered the needs of the associates and give them the support that they need to do their work. Their personal goals and views are taken into consideration by management. Rather than exercising authority, Robson and Jim have demonstrated humility to their associates (Figure 84).

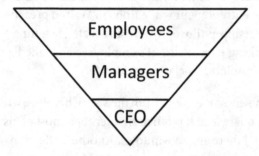

Figure 84: Servant Leadership Model

Highlights of the servant leadership model are as follows:

1) Employees are given the resources to create a healthy working environment. Happy employees are more motivated to serve customers better, resulting in higher customers' satisfaction.
2) Managers have an open mind to listen to the needs of employees.
3) CEO as a motivator, guardian, mentor, change agent, strategist and visionary.

The servant leadership model overlaps much of the teachings of Buddhism. Both focus on qualities such as selflessness, empathy, listening, serving others, awareness, and humility.

Below are some of Buddhism's quotes which are applicable to servant leadership:

Speech:

> "Whatever words we utter should be chosen with care for people will hear them and be influenced by them for good or ill."

> "The tongue like a sharp knife ... Kills without drawing blood."

Selflessness:

> "To live a pure unselfish life, one must count nothing as one's own in the midst of abundance."

Humility:

> "He who gives away shall have real gain. He who subdues himself shall be free; he shall cease to be a slave of passions. The righteous man casts off evil, and by rooting out lust, bitterness, and illusion do we reach Nirvana."

Motivation:

> "Thousands of candles can be lighted from a single candle, and the life of the candle will not be shortened. Happiness never decreases by being shared."

> "He is able who thinks he is able."

Empathy:

> "Have compassion for all beings, rich and poor alike; each has their suffering. Some suffer too much, others too little."

Case of Airbnb's Brian Chesky

Airbnb is a peer-to-peer online homestay platform where people are able to list and rent short-term accommodations. The company has more than 2 million listings in 34,000 countries and 191 countries. The company was founded in 2008 by Brian Chesky and Joe Gebbia. As of September 2016, the company was valued at around USD30 billion.

Much of the growth of the company is due to the willingness of its CEO, Brian Chesky, to learn from other successful CEOs. He sought their advice on growing Airbnb business. These are some of the lessons he learnt from them:

1) From Jonathan Ive, Chief Design Officer, Apple: *Stay focus*
2) From Bob Iger, CEO, Disney: *Stay cool*
3) From Warren Buffet, CEO, Berkshire Hathaway: *Avoid "noises" (distractions)*
4) From Sheryl Sandberg, COO, Facebook: *Ask questions*
5) From George Tenet, Former director of CIA: *Be visible*

Brian Chesky looks for certain qualities in his employees. They have to be dreamers, big thinkers, daring to take challenges, and trusting. They are kids at heart in terms of curiosity.

In order to attract more home owners to rent out their homes, Brian Chesky regards them as "partners". Guests are referred to as "customers". An online and in-person training course called *Hospitality Moments of Truth* is provided for each partner. Airbnb recognises the contribution of its partners through large conventions, where awards such as *Super Hosts* are given out to those who consistently meet targets set by the company.

Airbnb has taken the Oriental concept of building *guanxi* a step further by creating a marketplace where trust is built between strangers:

the hosts and the customers. Through reviews and ratings of hosts and ensuring security in financial transactions through payment gateways, the company seeks to reassure both parties that digital tools are as effective as face-to-face interactions (Figure 85).

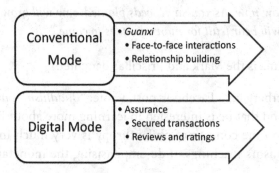

Figure 85: Building Relationship — Conventional versus Digital Mode

Case of Facebook's Mark Zuckerberg

Mark Zuckerberg, CEO of Facebook, was named as Fortune's Businessperson of 2016. Facebook has nearly 16,000 employees and is worth around USD350 billion. Mark Zuckerberg is estimated to have a net worth of USD51.2 billion as of June 2016.

Mark Zuckerberg, a Jewish — together with his physician wife, Priscilla Chan, a Buddhist — has become one of the world's most generous philanthropists. In a filing with the U.S. Securities and Exchange Commission, he announced his plans to sell or gift up to USD3 billion of Facebook stocks over a three-year period to an initiative to cure, prevent and manage diseases.

Another renowned philanthropist couple, Bill and Melinda Gates of Microsoft, commended Mark Zuckerberg and Priscilla Chan on their generosity. They said:

> "*The example you're setting today is an inspiration to us and the world. We can be confident of this: Maxima and every child born today will grow up in a world that is better than the one we know now. As you say, 'Seeds planted now will grow'. Your work will bear fruit for many decades to come.*"

(Maxima is the Mark and Priscilla's daughter.)

Zuckerberg, in a Facebook post, wrote: "*Buddhism is an amazing religion*" and that he is interested in learning more about Buddhism. His view on the concept of philanthropy is very much in line with the Buddhism's teachings of de-emphasising the monetary aspects of giving.

The Buddhist perspective on philanthropy embodies the pursuit of seeking *paramitas* (perfections or completeness). The seeking of *paramitas* is applied to all aspects of life including the practice of *dana* (generosity). In Buddhism, the path to enlightenment is a process of cultivation within one's being and reduces his selfishness and craving. Philanthropy benefits the giver from a spiritual perspective as well as the receiver from a pragmatic perspective. In Buddhism, there are six virtues or *paramitas* and one should practise to bring one to enlightenment (Figure 86).

Patience, is another *paramita* advocated by Mark Zuckerberg. When Facebook paid USD1 billion to acquire photo-sharing site Instagram in 2012, the company was less than two years old and had no revenue. Instagram's revenue is expected to exceed USD3 billion in 2016. With patience, Facebook hopes to replicate similar success with WhatsApp which it acquired for USD19 billion in 2014.

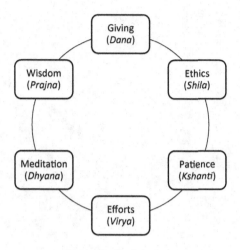

Figure 86: Six *Paramitas*

Concluding Remarks

This book focuses on the different paradigms of Chinese, Japanese and Korean management systems through theories and case studies. Readers will now be able to understand the varieties of management styles and the influences of cultures and philosophical beliefs on many business leaders.

Western management theories are designed with transactional efficiency in mind. Oriental management practices emphasise ethical codes, relations and family values. For Western managers to establish long-lasting relationships and build mutual trust with Oriental managers, they have to understand the key elements of Oriental business cultures and the complexities of negotiating with their counterparts in the East.

References

Abbe, A. & Halpin, S. (2009). The Cultural Imperative for Professional Military Education and Leader Development, *Parameters*, 20–31.

Albaum, G., Yu, J., Wiese, N., Hersche, J., Evangelista, F. & Murphy, B. (2010). Culture-based Values and Management Style of Marketing Decision Makers in Six Western Pacific Rim Countries. *Journal of Global Marketing 23*, 139–151.

Aycan, Z. (2006). Paternalism: Towards conceptual refinement and operationalization. In U. Kim, K.S. Yang, & K.K. Hwang (Eds.), *Indigenous and Cultural Psychology: Understanding People in Context.* 445–466. New York: Springer Science.

Bae, J. & Lawler, J.J. (2000). Organizational Performance and HRM Strategies in Korea: Impact on Firm Performance in an Emerging Economy. *Academy of Management Journal 43*(3), 502–517.

Beebee, S.A. & Mottet, T.P. (2010). *Business and Professional Communication: Principles and Skills for Leadership.* Boston, Massachusetts: Allyn & Bacon.

Bian Q. & Forsythe S. (2012). Purchase Intention for Luxury Brands: A Cross Cultural Comparison. *Journal of Business Research 65*(10), 1443–1451.

Cao, Y.F. & Li, P.P. (2010). Indigenous Research on Chinese Leadership: Problems and Suggestions. *Chinese Journal of Management 7*(11), 1704–1709.

Cameron, K., Freeman, S. & Mishra, A. (1991). Best Practices in White-collar Downsizing: Managing Contradictions. *Academy of Management Executive 5*, 57–73.

Carl, D., Gupta, V. & Javidan, M. (2004). Power distance. In R.J. House, P.J. Hanges, M. Javidan, P.W. Dorfman, & V. Gupta (Eds.), *Culture, Leadership, and Organizations: The GLOBE Study of 62 Cultures.* 513–563. Thousand Oaks, California: Sage.

Case, R. (2014). Divide and Conquer: When and Why Leaders Undermine the Cohesive Fabric of Their Group. *Journal of Personality and Social Psychology 7*(6), 1033–1050.

Chen, M. (2004). *Asian Management Systems: Chinese, Japanese and Korean Styles of Business*, Cengage Learning EMEA.

Cheung, C. & Chan, A. (2005). Philosophical Foundations of Eminent Hong Kong Chinese CEOs' Leadership. *Journal of Business Ethics 60*, 47–62.

Cheung, C. & Chan, A. (2008). Benefits of Hong Kong Chinese CEO's Confucian and Daoist Leadership Styles. *Leadership & Organization Development Journal 29*(6), 474–503.

Chinta, R. & Capar N. (2007). Comparative Analysis of Managerial Values in the USA and China. *Journal of Technology Management in China 2*(3), 212–224.

Cho, Y.H., & Yoon, J. (2001). The Origin and Function of Dynamic Collectivism: An Analysis of Korean Corporate Culture, *Asia Pacific Business Review 7*(4), 70–88.

Choi, T. & Nakano, C. (2008). The Evolution of Business Ethics in Japan and Korea over the Last Decade. *Human System Management 27*, 183–199.

Chung, K.H., Lee, H.C. & Jung, K.H. (1997). *Korean Management: Global Strategy and Cultural Transformation*. Berlin/New York: Walter de Gruyter.

Connor, J., Min, Y. & Iyengar, R. (2013). When East Meets West: A Global Merger between U.S. & Chinese Companies Required the Development of a Leadership Philosophy That Combines Eastern and Western Cultures. *T+D 67*(4), 54.

Conti, R., Angelis, J., Cooper, C., Faragher, B. & Gill, C. (2006). The Effects of Lean Production on Worker Job Stress. *International Journal of Operations & Production Management (26)*9, 1013–1038.

Dwyer, R.F., Schurr, P.H. & Oh, S. (1987). Developing Buyer-Seller Relationships. *Journal of Marketing 51*(2), 11–27.

Fan. P.K. & Zhang Z.K. (2004). Cross-cultural Challenges When Doing Business in China. *Singapore Management Review 26*(1), 81–90.

Fast, N.J., Halevey, N. & Galinsky, A.D. (2012). The Destructive Nature of Power without Status. *Journal of Experimental Social Psychology 48*, 391–394.

Fenby, J. (2013). *The History of Modern China: The Fall and Rise of a Great Power, 1850 to the Present*, 2nd edition. London, England: Penguin.

Francesco, A.M. & Gold B.A. (2005). *International Organizational Behavior: Text, Cases, and Skills*, 2nd edition. Upper Saddle River, New Jersey: Pearson Prentice Hall.

Gabarino, E. & Johnson, M.S. (1999). The Different Roles of Satisfaction, Trust and Commitment in Customer Relationships. *Journal of Marketing 63*(2), 70–87.

Gao, J-S., Arnulf, J.K. & Kristofferson, H. (2011). Western Leadership Development and Chinese Managers: Exploring the Need for Contextualization. *Scandinavian Journal of Management 27*, 55–65. http://dx.doi.org/10.1016/j.scaman.2010.11.007

Gulati, R., Huffman, S. & Neilson, G. (2008). *The Barista Principle — Starbucks and the Rise of Relational Capital*. Retrieved from http://www.relationalcapitalgroup.com/downloads/TheBaristaPrincple.pdf

Hartley, J., Jacobson, D., Klandermans, B. & van Vuuren, T. (1991). *Job Insecurity: Coping with Jobs at Risk*. London, England: Sage.

Hofstede, G. (1980). *Culture's Consequences: International Differences in Work-related Values*, London, England: Sage.

Hofstede, G. (1983a). National Cultures in Four Dimensions: A Research-based Theory of Cultural Differences among Nations. *International Studies of Management and Organization 13*(1), 46–74.

Hofstede, G. (1983b). The Cultural Relativity of Organizational Practices and Theories. *Journal of International Business Studies, 14*(2), 75–89.

Hofstede, G. & Bond, M. (1988). The Confucius Connection: From Cultural Roots to Economic Growth. *Organizational Dynamics 16*(4), 4–21.

Hofstede, G. (2001). *Culture's Consequences: Comparing Values, Behaviours, Institutions and Organizations across Nations,* 2nd edition. Thousand Oaks, California: Sage Publications, Inc.

Jeong Y. (2000). A paradigm shift of Korean HRM. In *Human Resource Management in the 21st Century.* Korea Labour Institute (Ed.). 33–54. Seoul, South Korea: Myung-Kyung Publishing Company.

Johnson. C. (1998). Why Managers Need to Think Globally. *HR Magazine,* April, 2–7.

Jung, D., Chan, F., Chen, G. & Chow, C. (2010). Chinese CEOs' Leadership Styles and Firm Performance. *Journal of Asia Business Studies 4*(2), 73–79.

Kenna, P. & Sondra, L. (1995). *Business Korea: A Practical Guide to Understand South Korean Business Culture,* Lincolnwood, Illinois: Passport Books.

Kets de Vries, M.F.R., & Balazs, K. (1997). The Downside of Downsizing. *Human Relations 50,* 11–50.

Khatri, N. (2009). Consequences of Power Distance Orientation in Organisations. *VISION-The Journal of Business Perspective 13*(1), 1–9.

Kirkbirde, P.S., Tang, S.F.Y. & Westwood, R.I. (1991). Chinese Conflict Preferences and Negotiating Behaviour: Cultural and Psychological Influences. *Organization Studies, 12,* 365–386.

Kotler, K. & Singh, R. (1981), Marketing Warfare in the 1980s, *The Journal of Business Strategy 1*(3), 30–41.

Lee, M.J. & Lee, D.H (2015). Effects of HPWSs on Employee' Attitude for Korean Firms: The Mediating Role of Human Resource Competency and the Moderating Role of Organization Culture. *Journal of Applied Business Research 31*(6), 2225–2236.

Lim, T. (2009). Face in the holistic and relativistic society. In F. Bargiela-Chiappini, M. Haugh (Eds.). *Face, Communication and Social Interaction,* London, England: Equinox.

Martinsons, M.G. (2001). *Comparing the Decision Styles of American, Chinese and Japanese Business Leaders,* Best Paper Proceedings of the Academy of Management Meetings, Washington, DC.

Matous, P. & Yasuyuki, T. *"Dissolve the Keiretsu, or Die": A Longitudinal Study of Disintermediation in the Japanese Automobile Manufacturing Supply Networks.* RIETI Discussion Paper Series 15-E-039, April 2015.

Nagashima, H. (1993). *A Reversed World or Is It? The Japanese Way of Communicating and Their Attitudes Towards Other Cultures,* Kyoto, Japan: Ritsumeikan University Press.

Nakamura, M., Shaver, J.M. & Yeung, B. (1996). An Empirical Investigation of Joint Venture Dynamics: Evidence from U.S.-Japan Joint Ventures. *International Journal of Industrial Organization 14*(4), 521–541.

Naude, P. & Buttle, F. (2000). Assessing Relationship Quality. *Industrial Marketing Management 29*(4), 351–361.

Nicholls-Nixon, C.L. & Woo, C.Y. (2003). Technology Sourcing and Output of Established Firms in a Regime of Encompassing Technological Change. *Strategic Management Journal 24*(7), 651–666.

Pascale, R.T. & Athos, A.G. (1981). The Art of Japanese Management. *Business Horizons, 24*(6), 83–85.

Paul, S., Seetharaman, P., Samarah, I., and Mykytyn, P.P. (2004). Impact of Heterogeneity and Collaborative Conflict Management Style on the Performance of Synchronous Global Virtual Teams. *Information and Management, 41*, 303–321.

Pellegrini, E.K. & Scandura, T.A. (2008). Paternalistic Leadership: A Review and Agenda for Future Research. *Journal of Management 34*(3), 566–593.

Rowe, A.J. & Boulgarides, J.D. (1983). Decision Styles — A Perspective. *Leadership and Organization Development Journal 4*(4), 3–9.

Rowe, A.J. & Boulgarides, J.D. (1994). *Managerial Decision Making*, Englewood Cliffs, New Jersey: Prentice-Hall.

Rowley, C. & Jun, I.W. (2013). Changes and Continuity in Management Systems and Corporate Performance: Human Resource Management, Corporate Culture, Risk Management and Corporate Strategy in South Korea. *Business History 56*(3), 485–508.

Rowley, C. & Bae J. (2013). Human resource management in South Korea. In *Managing Human Resource in Asia Pacific*. A. Varma & S. Budwar (Eds). 31–63. London, England: Routledge.

Rue, L.W. & Byars, L. (2003). *Management, Skills and Application*, 10th edition, New York: McGraw-Hill/Irwin, 259.

Scaborough, J. (1988). Comparing Chinese and Western Culture Roots: Why East Is East and West Is West. *Business Horizons 41*(6), 15–24.

Sethi., S.P. & Namiki, N. (1984). Japanese-style consensus decision-making in Matrix management: Problems and prospects of adaptation. In *Matrix Management Systems Handbook*. In D.I. Cleland (Ed.). 431–456. New York: Van Nostrand.

Thomas, K.W. & Kilmann, R.H. (1974). *Thomas-Kilmann Conflict Mode Instrument*, Palo Alto, California: Consulting Psychologists Press.

Tian, Q. (2008). Perception of Business Bribery in China: The Impact of Moral Philosophy. *Journal of Business Ethics 80*(3), 437–445.

Top 10 chaebol take up half of stock market cap. (2016, March 8). *The Korea Herald*. Retrieved from http://m.koreaherald.com/view.php?ud=20160808000666#jyk

Tung, R.L. (1998). *The New Expatriates: Managing Human Resources Abroad*, Cambridge, Massachusetts: Ballinger Publishing.

United Nations Conference on Trade and Development. *World Investment Report 2016: Annex Tables*, http://unctad.org/en/Pages/DIAE/World%20Investment%20Report/Annex-Tables.aspx

Wagner, R. & Harter, J.K. (2006). *12: The Elements of Great Managing*, New York: Gallup Press.

Wang, C.L., Ding, D.T. & Pervaiz, K.A. (2012). Entrepreneurial Leadership and Context in Chinese Firms: A Tale of Two Chinese Private Enterprises. *Asia Pacific Business Review 18*(4), 505–530.

Warner, M. (2009). 'Making sense' of HRM in China: Setting the Scene. *International Journal of Human Resource Management 20*(11), 2169–2193.

Warner, M. (2010). In Search of Confucian HRM: Theory and Practice in Greater China and Beyond. *The International Journal of Human Resource Management, 21*(12), 2053–2078.

Weber, J. (2001). Illusions of Marketing Planners. *Psychology & Marketing 18*(6), 527–563.

Webster, V., Myors, B. & Brough, P. (2011). The Dark Side of Leadership: The relationship between Self-management and the Tendency to Use Derailing Leadership Behaviour. *The Abstracts of the 9th Industrial and Organisational Psychology Conference held in Auckland, New Zealand.* Retrieved from https://www.psychology.org.au/Assets/Files/Combined-Abstracts-of-2011-Australian-Psychology-Conferences.pdf

Xing, Y. & Sims, D. (2012). Leadership, Daoist Wu Wei and Reflexivity: Flow, Self-protection and Excuse in Chinese Bank Managers' Leadership Practice. *Management Learning 43*(1), 97–112.

Xu, Y. & Zhang, B. (2007). *Mencius: A Benevolent Saint for the Ages*, Beijing, China: China Intercontinental Press.

Yen, A. & Barnes, B.R. (2011). Analyzing Stage and Duration of Anglo-Chinese Business-to-Business Relationships. *Industrial Marketing Management 40*(3), 346–357.

Yu, S.O. (2016). Reexamining Education Research Methodologies — Collaborative Rather Than Competitive. *Bulgarian Journal of Science and Education Policy, 10*(1), 124–141.

Index